DATE DUE

D1472335

THE
MANAGER'S
STEP-BY-STEP
GUIDE TO
OUTSOURCING

THE MANAGER'S STEP-BY-STEP GUIDE TO OUTSOURCING

LINDA R. DOMINGUEZ

McGraw-Hill
New York   Chicago   San Francisco
Lisbon   London   Madrid   Mexico City   Milan
New Delhi   San Juan   Seoul   Singapore
Sydney   Toronto

1 2 3 4 5 6 7 8 9 0   DOC/DOC   0 9 8 7 6 5

ISBN 0-07-145824-7

McGraw-Hill books are available at special quantity discounts to use as premiums and sales promotions, or for use in corporate training programs. For more information, please write to the Director of Special Sales, McGraw-Hill Professional, Two Penn Plaza, New York, NY 10121-2298. Or contact your local bookstore.

 This book is printed on recycled, acid-free paper containing a minimum of 50% recycled, de-inked fiber.

Library of Congress Cataloging-in-Publication Data

Dominguez, Linda R.
        The manager's step-by-step guide to outsourcing / by Linda R. Dominguez.
            p.   cm.
        1. Contracting out   2. Contracting out–Management.   I. Title.

    HD2365.D66   2005
    658.4'058—dc22   2005020850

For Josh, Joe, Denyse, Natascha, Anthony, Gabe, and Gavin – the loves of my life.

CONTENTS

ACKNOWLEDGMENTS   ix

INTRODUCTION   x

PART 1 • The Fundamentals   1

Chapter 1 • Welcome to the World of Outsourcing   5

Chapter 2 • Recent Surveys about Outsourcing
That Affect Your Business Decisions   17

PART 2 • Benefits and Barriers   27

Chapter 3 • Measuring the Risks and Rewards   29

Chapter 4 • Determining What to Outsource   45

Chapter 5 • Critical Success Factors
in Vendor Selection   59

Chapter 6 • Transition Blueprint   75

PART 3 • Commitment to Succeed   91

Chapter 7 • Building Your Team   93

CONTENTS

Chapter 8 • New Skills Needed   105

Chapter 9 • Critical Success Factors for Managers   123

Chapter 10 • Outsourcing Hurdles and
               How to Overcome Them   135

Chapter 11 • Dealing with Cultural and
               Language Barriers   147

PART 4 • The Balancing Act   159

Chapter 12 • Balancing the Needs   161

Chapter 13 • Exit Management   171

PART 5 • No Surprises   183

Chapter 14 • Success Factors for Outsourcing   185

Chapter 15 • Resources for Success   193

APPENDIX   THE EFFECT OF OUTSOURCING AND
             OFFSHORING ON BLS PRODUCTIVITY
             MEASURES   207

INDEX   221

ACKNOWLEDGMENTS

So many people helped me in the creation of this book, and I would like to thank them. First, thanks to Phil Hatch, president of Ventoro.com, who generously shared his wisdom, research, and opinions. Second, thanks to all of those kind and helpful people who abundantly shared their knowledge and tips: Art Salyer, Rick Friedrich, Brad Peterson, Brian Mahoney, Geoff Smith, Paul Laudicina, Adam Kolawa, Binod Taterway, George Spafford, Linda Cohen, Larry Ponemon, Dick LeFave, David D'Innocenzo, Lilia Tsalalikhin, Mike Matteo, and Scott Nobel. Thanks too, to the kind folks at Accenture, ADP, and Kelly Services.

And especially, thanks to Donya Dickerson, my editor at McGraw-Hill, who understood how to motivate me to get the words on the paper.

Thank you all for your generous help.

INTRODUCTION

out·sourc·ing
Pronunciation: "owt-sOr-sing"
Function: noun
: The practice of subcontracting work to
an outside vendor
: One hot potato

The issue of outsourcing is one of the most difficult and controversial topics in the business world today, often further complicated by unrealistic expectations of cost savings and fast returns on investments. It is time to dispel the common myths about outsourcing, and to develop a strategy that organizations can use as a platform to enthusiastically welcome and support the opportunity to reduce costs; increase productivity, innovation, and service; and generate higher returns for shareholders.

While coaching executives and corporations over the last several years, I became aware of an interesting trend in outsourcing. In part, I found that the terms *outsourcing* and *offshoring* were being used interchangeably, when, in fact, they are two very different things. I also found that the most successful outsourcing projects, on- or offshore, shared certain fundamental traits—primarily that the executives of successful projects were exceptional leaders, and that these leaders created success through a complete pre-project, in-house situational diagnosis before moving on to an even more comprehensive evaluation of the outsourcing process.

As an executive coach, I share resources, opportunities, possibilities, information, and guidance with my clients, and this book is designed to provide those same elements to organizations, large or small, that want to learn more about achieving success through an outsourcing initiative.

In this book, I share the guidance and counsel of my clients as well as the advice of experts, and through these people you will learn that when executives limit their outsourcing considerations and decisions to cost reduction alone, the outcome is usually failure. Successful outsourced business units and functions are developed through a combination of *best-approach* methodologies along with continued collaboration with a well-prepared leadership team, supported by external experts on issues that extend far beyond the anticipated financial rewards. Sustained success requires a first-class leader and a first-rate, comprehensive strategy.

When considering a decision to outsource any business unit or function, companies and their leaders must weigh the potential cost savings against the potential risks—and the potential risks are abundant. This book provides you with the guidance you need on the essential issues that must be addressed if the fundamental structure of your outsourcing strategy and its implementation is to be sound. As you read this book, you will find insights into the problems and challenges you are likely to face, with detailed advice on how to anticipate, mitigate, and manage those problems and challenges. As a peer-to-peer guide for executives, this book includes contributions from executives who have successfully outsourced, and also from those who found that their projects did not meet their expectations. It also provides sound advice, tips, and tools for organizations considering outsourcing on- or offshore, with guidelines on how to plan and implement the process successfully, allowing each reader to apply practical, topical, and timely recommendations to his or her circumstances:

For the executive: Why consider an outsourcing initiative, and why now? Learn what you need to know before you make your decision.

For the manager: Learn the major hurdles that management must overcome, the new skills needed to deliver results on time and on budget, and tips on maintaining control of the project and the trust of your staff.

For vendor selection: Learn how to select the best vendor for your specific needs (and get tips on how to avoid the charlatans).

Making it work: Learn how to help your team through the change in culture and dynamics that will take place, how to make your outsourcing initiative successful, how to avoid the most common outsourcing blunders, and what to do when it's "too late."

As a reference guide, this book examines the reasons behind the successes that organizations have achieved, allowing you to analyze their decision drivers, questions, research, and considerations when developing your own plan.

For executives, managers, consultants, service vendors, and employees around the world—for anyone who is currently involved in or considering an outsourcing initiative—the concepts and strategies defined in this book will help you take an objective view of your own circumstances, opportunities, barriers—and choices. They will guide you to informed, strategic decisions so that you can experience sustained success in your outsourcing project.

In Part 1 you will learn the fundamentals of outsourcing, including standard buzzwords and definitions. We asked experts from around the globe for their input. Before we uncover the best practices used by executives in creating and managing any outsourcing process, you will read results from the most recent studies and surveys on outsourcing, including market share statistics, outsourcing decision factors, partner and vendor selection statistics, and results of surveys capturing the human element and the impact on the retained team and staff. Reviewing these data will help you easily determine which of these factors are critical to the success of your own outsourcing initiative.

Part 2 introduces more complex issues: the benefits and barriers surrounding outsourcing, along with "how to's" from experts in the field. In addition to learning the real risks and rewards of implementing an outsourcing initiative, you will learn how to choose what to outsource, critical issues to consider in vendor or service vendor selection, and how to create a blueprint for your own outsourcing success.

Part 3 is real-time advice on making an outsourcing project succeed: What are the new skills that executives, managers, and employees must learn if they are to deliver results? This section defines those new skills, presents typical implementation hurdles, and presents tips for overcoming those hurdles. In addition to building a strong and cohesive team, one critical issue in any outsourcing situation is culture; managing an outsourcing project across town can be a challenge, and when the project is offshore, the cultural and language barriers must be navigated carefully. Part 3 provides you with insights on identifying and understanding cultural and style differences and letting them move you forward rather than hold you back.

Part 4 tackles the paradox created by outsourcing in balancing the present and future agendas of shareholders, vendors, managers, employees, and customers. You will learn best practices for creating sustainable shareholder value, without sacrificing quality, productivity, relationships, or control. This section also addresses the steps to take when you must bring an outsourced business unit back in-house. Developing and implementing an effective exit strategy requires a close and continuous legal overview, and this chapter will provide readers with the key issues and recommendations from leading legal experts in the field.

Part 5 summarizes the concepts in this book, and provides a list of additional resources for further information.

Throughout this book, you will read vivid examples of others who have successfully wrestled with the cycles of harmony and disorder in the outsourcing process. You will have an opportunity to examine outsourcing success from several angles, and to apply the concepts and strategies to your specific situation, so that you can define your own success.

Use this book as your road map for creating successful outsourcing initiatives for your organization—you will avoid the pitfalls and achieve success much more quickly than you thought possible.

PART 1

THE FUNDAMENTALS

If you are going to create a successful, long-term outsourcing program, you must begin at the beginning, the *very* beginning. This section provides the buzzwords and acronyms used in outsourcing, enabling you to understand the vendors and salespeople that will come your way (and they will come; once the word is out, you will be fair game!).

This section also provides you with a comprehensive understanding of outsourcing and offshoring so that you can *begin* to determine if this will be a wise option for your organization. To help you with the initial determining factors, this section also provides you with the most recent survey data concerning outsourcing decision drivers, outsourcing markets, successes, failures, and more. Use these data to complete your understanding of the options available through outsourcing; then you can move forward into the selection process.

GLOSSARY OF TERMS, ACRONYMS, AND ABBREVIATIONS

The following glossary of terms, acronyms, and abbreviations should help you to become familiar with some of the terms used in the world of outsourcing.

BPO   Business process outsourcing

BTO   Business transformation outsourcing

CMM   Capabilities maturity model

CRM   Customer relationship management

CSF   Critical success factors

CSR   Corporate social responsibility

CSV   Creating shareholder value

DT   Decision team

ERM   Employee relationship management

ERP   Enterprise resource planning

EVA   Economic value add

FTE   Full-time equivalent

FUD   Fear, uncertainty, and doubt

IPR   Intellectual property rights

ISO   International standard operations

KPI   Key performance indicators

M&A   Mergers and acquisitions

MMR   Monitor, measure, and report

MSA   Master service agreement

MSE   Multisource environment

MSU   Making stuff up

OBE	Overcome by events
ODC	Offshore dedicated center
OLA	Operating-level agreement
OMT	Operations management team
PMI	Program Management Institute
PMO	Project management office
RFA	Request for application
RFI	Request for information
RFP	Request for proposal
ROI	Return on investment
ROO	Return on outsourcing
SLA	Service-level agreement
SMB	Small and midsized business market
SMO	Service management office
SOW	Statement of work
SVM	Shareholder value management
TCO	Total cost of outsourcing
TU	True-up
VBM	Values-based management
VST	Vendor selection team

CHAPTER 1

WELCOME
TO THE WORLD
OF OUTSOURCING

WHAT IS OUTSOURCING?

Outsourcing is the practice of hiring functional experts to handle business units that are outside of your firm's core business. It is also a method of staff augmentation without adding to head count. *Offshoring*, or outsourcing offshore, is the practice of hiring experts in other countries to handle business processes that may be outside of your core business focus, or to reduce costs, enhance quality, and improve productivity. The world of outsourcing, onshore or offshore, may simply be described as delegating at an intercompany level rather than an intracompany level.

In order for you to make an informed decision about any outsourcing program, there are specific steps you must take to ensure success. A great way to understand the complex scope of outsourcing is through a little history.

OUTSOURCING ONSHORE, OFF-SITE

Using outsourcing as a business strategy is not new. Decades ago, ADP (Automatic Data Processing) led the way to what is now considered onshore, off-site outsourcing.

After World War II, the federal debt rose to the then-astounding peak of $279 billion. By 1949, the federal government was finding new ways to pay off the debt, including the withholding of employee income taxes, and the burden on the employer of properly calculating, withholding, and keeping track of these dollars through payroll expanded. ADP realized that its expertise in payroll and taxes could be offered to other companies without such expertise, and it began offering companies the opportunity to outsource their payroll functions by simply delivering a copy of their payroll roster to ADP. ADP keypunch operators entered the data, and payroll checks, with appropriate withholding and recordkeeping, were returned to the company in time for payday.

ADP knew 50 years ago that companies that made cars, packaged consumer goods, built machines, or provided customer services all had core areas of business expertise, but payroll was not one of them. The more complicated payroll became, the larger ADP's market became, making ADP one of the pioneers of onshore, off-site outsourcing.

OUTSOURCING ONSHORE, ON-SITE

With an office in Detroit, Michigan, and two employees, William Russell Kelly started a company to meet the office and clerical needs of Detroit-area businesses by providing calculating and inventory services, typing and copying. Initially customers sent their work to Mr. Kelly's office, but as customers gained confidence in the new company, they began asking Mr. Kelly to send his employees to their offices to type, file, or operate business machines. Over 50 years ago, Mr. Kelly understood the importance of companies playing to their strengths. The company known in 1946 as Russell Kelly Office Services led the way in outsourcing onshore, on-site; it is now known as Kelly Services, a Fortune 500 company that is going strong.

OUTSOURCING OFFSHORE

While the practice of offshoring began decades ago (for example, Nike in the 1970s), offshoring gained steam in the 1980s and 1990s as companies increased the outsourcing of lower-level, repetitive back-office jobs to onshore organizations that could do the work more efficiently and cost-effectively. Later in the 1990s, United States companies began hiring programmers in other countries, primarily India, to help corporate America in its race against the dreaded Y2K deadline. This need, along with the simultaneous expansion of the Internet and the telecommunications industry, made doing work remotely far less expensive and far more efficient.

While onshore outsourcing is a method by which companies can hand over work to others who can do it inexpensively through gaining greater economies of scale, offshore outsourcing, or offshoring, is the process of outsourcing functions and business units to workers and business partners who are both outside the work site and outside the United States. As the global economy chugs along, companies that want to achieve high performance must balance the need for efficient operations with the need to deliver on current earnings. In order to do both, organizations must invest in future growth that will create new shareholder value. Does this automatically point to outsourcing a business unit offshore? Maybe—but maybe not.

Before discussing whether your firm should consider outsourcing as a strategy, let's first take a closer look at why organizations typically choose to outsource.

WHY OUTSOURCE?

Rapidly changing and increasingly complex business issues are creating key shifts in organizations and the manner in which they do business. The advance of technology, the sophistication of business operations, and the need for constant growth are circumstances that suggest a focus on functional core competencies. As companies struggle to adapt to and keep up with the demands of customers and shareholders alike, that focus on core competencies may suggest outsourcing as a potential strategy to remain competitive.

A recent study of some five thousand executives conducted by Ventoro.com demonstrated that there are decision drivers for outsourcing that are valid, and other decision drivers that are a pathway to failure. Typically, outsourcing decision drivers fall into the following categories:

1. *To respond to a power play.* Whether the pressure to outsource is imposed by the board of directors, shareholders, or other senior management, coercion is the least effective primary decision driver. According to research conducted by Ventoro.com in 2004, almost 20 percent of the respondents stated that their outsourcing initiative was driven by pressure from shareholders, boards of directors, or C-level executives. A best-practice response to this pressure is to choose an outsourcing strategy only after first establishing that it is the best solution for your specific business requirements.

2. *To alleviate pain.* Pain can be a powerful motivator, and when pain in the form of operating challenges exists, it may be an appropriate driver for an outsourcing solution, specifically to

   • Reduce and control operating costs

- Reduce labor costs
- Balance competitive pressure

Tip: When a business process is in trouble while it is still in-house (that is, when the process is broken), shuttling it off-site or offshore will just move the problem. Fix the problem first, then outsource off-site or offshore.

---

3. *To fill a need:* When you can envision the gap between where you are now, or *what is,* and where you want to be, or *what could be,* your decision drivers may be in this category.

- Improve company focus
- Achieve cost savings
- Achieve revenue goals through round-the-clock shifts
- Gain access to world-class capabilities
- Improve time to market
- Achieve development schedules not possible with internal staff
- Avoid historic problems with projects that have been difficult to manage
- Scale up for a project without increasing the number of permanent staff
- Create a global market for your product or service
- Improve efficiency
- Focus on core business
- Redirect your internal resources for other purposes
- Become truly customer focused
- Take advantage of potential tax incentives

Organizations that are experiencing pain will want to seek relief, and organizations with a need or desire will work to improve the status quo. Again, outsourcing may be the right move—but it may not be.

WHO SUCCEEDS, AND WHY

As a strategic business tool, outsourcing allows organizations to identify those functions that are not directly creating value for customers or shareholders (those that are not core business functions) and consider them as possible candidates for outsourcing. Depending on the strength of the foundation of your outsourcing initiative, outsourcing even the "good to go" business units may result in outcomes that aren't always successful. Here are some examples.

POTENTIAL OUTCOMES WITH A WEAK FOUNDATION

The objectives are not achieved because

- There was not enough precontract due diligence; the organization's expectations were unclear to the vendor.
- The implementation team or the ongoing management team was unprepared for the challenges of the new process.
- The implementation team lacked the skills, knowledge, and style required to succeed.
- The managing executive did not establish a performance baseline prior to sending the functions to the vendor.
- The client-vendor relationship was rushed; roles and responsibilities were unclear.

- Midcontract, the ongoing management team changed the scope of the project; the vendor agreed to the change in scope (but was unable to complete the project on time or on budget).

- Outsourcing was not the right solution in the first place.

- Internal support dissipated. (If the entire organization does not support the initiative, lowered morale will impede your progress.)

- There was a lack of communication or management in-house.

- There was a lack of proper project management.

- Decision making was delegated to the vendor.

- There were cultural, language, or communication issues with the vendor.

- The vendor simply failed to execute as expected.

The objectives are achieved, but

- The organization was displeased with the vendor relationship because of ethical issues.

- Brain drain left your company without key knowledge centers.

POTENTIAL OUTCOMES WITH A STRONG FOUNDATION

- Both client and vendor are satisfied with each other, and both benefited from the arrangement.

- The outsourcing arrangement achieved more benefits than anticipated at the outset.

- Both parties view the other as a "trusted partner" and continually work to create new opportunities to forge a deeper, more integrated relationship; share risks and rewards; and move their objectives to increasingly higher levels.

- Outsourcing resolved the organization's needs and desires.

Successful outsourcing initiatives begin with a strong foundation, executive support, a well-paced and comprehensive strategy, and a vision for success that serves all parties.

SUCCESS FOUNDATION, PART 1

Brian Maloney, the former COO of Perot Systems, was responsible for the company's market-facing activities, including its major vertical industry concentrations—financial services, health care, industrial services, and strategic markets—its global infrastructure support unit, and its consulting businesses. Maloney's success resulted from his ability to base the decision-making process on a return to value. In order to experience that return to value and the financial rewards associated with it, Maloney simply asked, "What does success look like? That is our starting point."

SUCCESS FOUNDATION, PART 2

Industry expert Geoff Smith, principal and founder of LP Enterprises, recommends that CIOs take a proactive view of their own operations, rather than waiting for the CEO or CFO to ask about the merits of outsourcing or offshoring. "At that point," Smith states, "you're playing defense." He also recommends that you take your time, as rushing into a project is a fast path to failure.

For 25 years, Smith was deputy CIO for Procter & Gamble (P&G), where he led a complex outsourcing initiative that spanned several years. Thinking strategically, P&G first identified the issues: Its information technology (IT) functions were decentralized; it needed to find ways to run globally; it wanted IT to become a strategic weapon rather than a cost center; and it needed to standardize for efficiencies.

As an example, Smith recalls that some 25 years ago, P&G developed an internal e-mail system, which R&D used to grow the best ideas for product development and manufacturing. In 1980, this was a strategic application; however, more recently P&G determined that running a world-class e-mail operation internally was no longer a competitive advantage. P&G outsourced that service to Hewlett-Packard as part of a large, multiyear outsourcing agreement signed in 2003.

The process at P&G did not begin with "what should we move?" Instead, the process began with the identification of P&G's core competencies. "P&G is all about understanding consumer needs," Smith states. At the end of the core business function identification, P&G found that IT infrastructure and enterprise applications were not on the core competencies list, nor was benefits administration and payroll or facilities management or accounts payable or human resources.

The company's next step was to create a Shared Services group in-house, some 7,000 strong, centralizing these services for the organization. From the day it started, P&G realized that Shared Services would eventually hit the ceiling, and that the company would then have to either take on outside business or outsource with a vendor who could offer greater efficiencies.

For a full year, P&G explored a complete business process outsourcing program, i.e., selling the assets and creating an equity position. While this model has been popular and successful in some cases, P&G decided it was not going to work for it, so it spent another full year exploring the possibility of outsourcing (on-site and off-site) its noncore functions. At the end of this lengthy due diligence process, it found the right answer for P&G, one that allowed it to transfer the majority of the 7,000 people in Shared Services to its outsourcing partners—these people would work at the same desks and do the same jobs, but would wear a different name badge.

Approximately half of P&G's IT organization was ultimately moved to Hewlett-Packard or IBM as part of this particular outsourcing initiative. While there were considerable and lengthy internal deliberations on where to draw the boundaries between what to keep and what to outsource, P&G decided which roles to move by looking through the eyes of customers such as Kroger or Wal-Mart or the consumers who buy the products. "If they couldn't 'see' the work or wouldn't pay extra for it, then it was a candidate for outsourcing. From there, we considered scale and natural synergies," Smith said.

RIGHTSOURCING

Clearly, both Brian Maloney and Geoff Smith understand the outsourcing decision-making process as strategic, building strong foundations on which to build their entire programs. In order to secure a successful outsourcing program, on- or offshore, leaders must ask and answer the following questions:

1. What is our definition of success?

2. Why are we even talking about this?

3. Is outsourcing right for us, and if so, why?

4. What should we outsource, and what must stay here?

5. Where should we outsource, on- or offshore?

6. How much will it cost?

7. How long will it take to implement?

8. How long will it take to realize our objectives in dollars?

9. What skills must remain here?

10. What skills are needed "there"?

11. What are the economic risks and rewards?

12. What cultural or language issues might exist?

13. What are the ethical issues (Sarbanes-Oxley-related) that we might encounter?

14. What are the tax advantages or disadvantages of an onshore or offshore outsourcing initiative?

15. What are the psychological effects on the retained and outsourced employees?

In the following chapters we will explore each of these questions, and others, to make sure that your decision drivers are sound, your foundation is strong, and your outsourcing efforts are successful.

CHAPTER 2

RECENT SURVEYS ABOUT OUTSOURCING THAT AFFECT YOUR BUSINESS DECISIONS

As you think about your own outsourcing needs and plans, there is a great deal that you can learn from the data that are currently available. Several surveys and studies on outsourcing and offshoring have recently been conducted. Some of the less-than-objective (and less-than-scientific) studies and surveys are often used by outsourcing consultants to drive your business to one of their partner companies offshore. The survey results presented here are the product of long-term studies conducted by objective parties—researchers with a balanced and realistic view of the landscape for outsourcing and offshoring.

Ventoro.com is an outsourcing research firm whose president, Phillip Hatch, compares the current outsourcing phenomenon to the Gold Rush of 1848 when General John Sutter found gold in Coloma, California. General Sutter was able to keep his find a secret for a short time, but once the rumor was out, people jumped at the chance to make their fortune in gold.

The people of the day listened to the rumors of gold just lying around for the taking, and they rushed off to California to build their financial empires. While it is true that a few individuals were able to amass substantial wealth during the height of the Gold Rush, most people never quite reached the levels of financial success they had come to expect. As Hatch states,

> The real story of the Gold Rush is not of wealth and riches, but of those people who jumped at the idea of easy fortunes without knowledge of how to find gold, how to mine for gold, or even how to survive in a wild and unsettled country. To make the challenge worse, these '49ers faced a constant barrage from swindlers claiming to offer "the secret" to mining success, preferred mining sites, near-magic tools, or an expedited journey to California. More often than not, these shady characters had little or no more experience than the prospectors they preyed upon.

The outsourcing market may be an example of history repeating itself. While organizations may be able to achieve significant cost reductions, many do not. Just as in the Gold Rush days, a failure to achieve outsourcing success is often caused by a lack of leadership, many misconceptions, unrealistic expectations of success, and a poor strategy. Organizations that launch an outsourcing initiative before completely developing and understanding their own definition of success often find failure knocking at their door.

I don't frown on outsourcing or offshoring—moving existing business functions to outsourced service providers is one of the most powerful tools an executive can use to improve both bottom-line and even top-line numbers. However, outsourcing must be done *after* establishing a sound business case and with a full understanding of the effort and planning it takes to be successful.

Hatch and his team launched an aggressive research project to get to the heart of what it takes to be a success story in outsourcing. Over 5,000 executives were surveyed across the globe, in countries including Germany, France, the United Kingdom, Italy, Canada, and of course the United States. The primary focus of this survey is offshore; however, U.S. domestic survey results are also reflected here.

HOW BIG IS OUTSOURCING: WHAT ARE FORECAST MODELS SAYING?

The Ventoro survey indicates that outsourcing—particularly offshore—is occurring at a much slower rate than is perceived by the public. When all respondents are considered, only 19 percent had a current offshore strategy. Nevertheless, when only those in the Fortune 1,000 ranks are considered, the number of firms engaged in an offshore strategy jumped significantly, to 95 percent. When asked about future outsourcing plans, only 32 percent of the participating executives indicated that they were planning an offshore initiative within the next 12 months ending December 2005.

Table 2.1: How Big is the Market

For all respondents

Have a current offshore strategy?	19%
Have no outsource strategy?	81%

Table 2.2: How Big is the Market

For Fortune 1000 firms

Have a current offshore strategy?	95%
Have no outsource strategy?	5%

WHY COMPANIES
CONSIDER OUTSOURCING

The Ventoro study found that the number one reason for outsourcing was in an effort to achieve cost savings. While improving quality, improving time to market, gaining new skills, improving cost predictability, increasing market penetration, and gaining new industry expertise also were cited as primary drivers for outsourcing, the worst reason for beginning an outsourcing initiative was because of *force*. Yet 19 percent of the respondents selected "by force" as one of their primary drivers—almost one in five executives. Ventoro, our experts, and our executives all agree that pursing an outsourcing strategy because of pressure from shareholders or the board without first proving that outsourcing is the best business solution is an opportunity to fail.

Table 2.3: Why Pursue Offshore?

Why move offshore?

Achieve cost savings	70%	Forced strategy	19%
Improve quality	49%	Cost predictability	11%
Improve time to market	40%	Penetrate market	9%
Gain technical skill sets	38%	Gain industry expertise	7%

WHY STAY ONSHORE?

Phillip Hatch of Ventoro states that when questioning those executives who rejected an outsourcing strategy (as opposed to those who began implementation, failed, and recalled the project in-house), the primary reasons to keep projects in-house were related to security (including IP theft and fraud) and quality issues. Of these executives, 80 percent cited security as their main concern, followed closely by quality issues at 74 percent. Ventoro's survey revealed that only one in three of the executives admitted that they would be willing to revaluate an outsourcing strategy if their apprehension over both security and quality could be adequately alleviated.

Table 2.4 Why Choose Not to Outsource?

Why stay onshore?

Security	80%
Quality	74%
Model didn't work	49%
Onshore employee concerns	42%
No customer support	19%
No business driver	18%
Better onshore options	9%

HOW WELL IS OUTSOURCING WORKING?

The Ventoro survey, focusing primarily on offshore outsourcing engagements, found the average cost savings (remember, this was the primary decision driver) to be just under 10 percent. The cost savings seems quite low until you take into account the number of engagements that actually increased costs (nearly 28 percent) and those that did not generate any material cost savings (25 percent).

When the "failed" engagements were removed, along with those outsourcing programs that had no prior baseline against which to compare cost savings, the average savings jumped to 19 percent—still very different from the highly touted opportunity to save 35 to 40 percent in costs.

REALITY CHECK

Hatch states,

> In our research, we found nearly 5 percent of those polled achieved a cost savings exceeding 50 percent. Upon further investigation, most of these firms had unusual circumstances related to their strategy, such as replacing a $400 per hour employee with another resource for $50 per hour. When we removed these firms from the equation, we found that only two firms out of all 5,000-plus organizations that we researched had achieved such a significant savings. Organizations anticipating an outsourcing or offshoring savings of 50 percent or more are not being realistic.

Table 2.5 What Is the Bottom-Line Success?

How well is it working?

Increase in costs	28%	21–40% savings	10%
No savings	25%	41–60%	4%
0–20% savings	30%	61% or more savings	1%

WHY DO THESE STRATEGIES FAIL?

Another point of consensus across the board: The ultimate success (or failure) of an outsourcing initiative is directly related to the performance of the organization's senior executives. Ventoro found that 52 percent of outsourcing engagements that failed did so because of problems exclusive to the leadership of the organization.

Table 2.6 Reasons for Failure

Why do strategies fail?

Organization preparation and execution	28%
Joint organization-vendor planning	21%
Vendor performance expectations	15%
Wrong answer	14%
Organization team morale and support	10%
Culture and communications	9%
Other	3%

The failure research and analysis compiled by Ventoro is straightforward: The leading cause of failure is a lack of preparation and/or execution by the organization. Hatch says,

The executive must prepare the organization well before the engagement. Then, the executive must set high standards for the vendor in terms of performance and detail to ensure that when you engage the vendor, you can verify that every detail is recorded, reviewed, and planned. As a general rule of thumb, the executive should be the one pushing for greater clarity throughout the entire engagement rather than waiting for the vendor to ask.

The second root cause of failure is condensed or incomplete planning, a result of the fast and furious trying to get contracts signed before the organization has had an opportunity to clarify roles, responsibilities, and expectations. The comprehensive planning of deliverables, operations, performance, metrics, and so on is the direct obligation of the managing executive.

Hatch states that while compiling the research, Ventoro found an alarming number of executives who would not accept accountability for the failure of their outsourcing strategy, no matter how closely they were working with their outsourcing team. An example of an executive statement regarding failure is:

> In the end there were too many gray areas, and our vendor wouldn't work with us to get this done.

which Hatch interprets to mean:

> I failed to adequately explain what we expected and what we needed prior to signing the contract.

Outsourcing strategies succeed or fail for many reasons, but ultimately it is up to the senior executive to make it happen. Success demands a strong strategy, learning new leadership skills so that you can create a path for your managers and vendors to follow.

A MACRO-MEGA TREND

Paul Laudicina, vice president and managing director of AT Kearney's Global Business Policy Council, has more than 20 years of consulting experience working with the leaders of corporations across a broad range of strategic and corporate policy issues. The author of the bestselling book *World out of Balance*, Mr. Laudicina states,

> My view of outsourcing in a broad context is that there is a demographic transition already underway, with difficult political issues in industrialized countries experiencing a labor surplus. Over time, projections within the United States and Europe is that we will be moving into another labor shortage by 2010—a shortage of somewhere between 6 and 7 million positions.

Laudicina, no stranger to globalization, shares that "tomorrow's decision will be whether to import labor or export jobs."

The reasons, he contends, fall in the fields of science and engineering. The Council on Innovation report indicates that we will have a spectacular shortage in science and engineering—yet the number of Americans going into computer science is dwindling. "It's perplexing," Laudicina states. "There is a decline in college freshmen intending to go into science fields, yet we face this potential shortage—and this shortage is compounded by the fact that we have a net decline in foreign students coming to this country."

Executives contemplating an outsourcing engagement must focus on demographic dynamics—the pain of outsourcing and offshoring will diminish as we return to a war for talent and focus globally, and as executives begin to focus on becoming more creative in sourcing domestically.

CONCLUSIONS

The trend among those firms that have higher outsourcing success rates indicates that organizations that take the time to do their homework and to build a business model for outsourcing *that works* were the most successful. Successful outsourcing engagements also require organizations that simply refuse to move a broken process or function, organizations that inform and include their teams and staff, organizations that realize that an outsourcing initiative takes time (P&G's entire process took *years*), and organizations that refuse to be pushed into signing a contract.

Organizations that are willing to take the time to complete a robust due-diligence process and assign a full-time team to consider all options, including demographics, politics, and best sourcing (regardless of location), always come up on top. Finally, the most successful outsourcing engagements are created and implemented by organizations whose executives accept complete responsibility for the success or failure of the process.

So, given all of this failure information, why would anyone consider an outsourcing initiative? Because of the potential rewards you can experience when you do it right.

PART 2

BENEFITS
AND BARRIERS

Outsourcing is not simply packing up IT jobs and shipping them overseas—it is much more than that, and it has been a staple of American corporations for years. When planned and executed well, an outsourcing initiative can be extremely successful. Take the Scotts Company, specifically its Miracle-Gro product line: When the Scotts Miracle-Gro brand was expanded to include bedding plants, Rick Friedrich, director of Scotts Branded Plants, worked with a network of growers across the country to select, grow, and ship the Scotts Miracle-Gro branded plants to retailers in the United States. Yes, Scotts outsourced the growing of the plants to vendors whose primary business was growing perfect plant material to the specifications of the Scotts Miracle-Gro brand. This outsourcing initiative continues to work well for the Scotts Company, due in large part to Friedrich's ability to monitor the details and manage for results. His expectations are clear to the growers, and he works closely with the growers to ensure that they understand what must be done, how well, and within what time frame.

Outsourcing has been a good business choice for the Scotts Company, being based on a solid business model and led by an executive who knows how to make those relationships work. Before jumping into this project, the Scotts

Company had to evaluate the risks and rewards, determine what and how to outsource, select the right growers, and put the right team together to make it work.

The following chapters will provide you with information on evaluating your possible risks and calculating potential rewards, a vendor selection template, and a transition blueprint so that your own outsourcing initiative can be as successful as that of the Scotts Company.

CHAPTER 3

MEASURING THE RISKS AND REWARDS

Twenty-five years ago, what we now call outsourcing was called *time-sharing*. This practice, the on- and offshore sub-contracting marketplace, has grown dramatically over the last several years, and will continue to do so as corporations focus on a return to value.

You might think that after 25 years, the process of defining and implementing an outsourcing initiative would be relatively simple and painless, that there would be no hurdles to overcome and no snags to work out, and that all of the risks associated with outsourcing would be mitigated to the point that an organization could easily create an outsourcing initiative that would deliver immediate results. Unfortunately, that is not the case—each outsourcing program, on- or offshore, differs in complexity, and each has its own set of risks and its own set of rewards that must be identified and measured.

If you can answer the question, "Why should we outsource?" with a hearty, "I don't know yet!" then you are on the right track. Your thorough and systematic due-diligence process will answer that question fully. A significant part of this investigative process must include a review of the risks and rewards experienced by those who have gone before.

THE RISKS

First, let's take a closer look at the risks, some of them clearly visible and some hidden, associated with an outsourcing initiative.

CUSTOMER SERVICE RISKS

I had to make a quick business trip to Houston from San Francisco recently, and I used an online travel service that I had used before with great success. Somehow, on this transaction, my credit card was charged twice, and it took me three hours via telephone to clear up the issue. Their call center has been outsourced to India—and the call center rep was polite and incompetent. I'll never use that online travel service again.

—CFO, SAN FRANCISCO

This scenario is not unique. If you outsource customer-facing functions, you must recognize the need to exercise close control over the processes that most directly affect your relationships with your current customers.

Your outsourcing initiative may be developed to create cost savings for shareholders, but when you outsource a customer-facing process, your success will be gained or lost on the basis of your customers' experience. Customers expect predictability. Insist that your outsourcing provider has the same commitment to service as you do; establish metrics for what you define to be "predictable," including service results; and measure your outsourcing provider against those metrics regularly.

> *Key point:* Keep the value close to your customers.

PRIVACY AND SECURITY RISKS

UCSF Med Center had a 20-year relationship with an onshore, off-site medical transcription service. While the Med Center was aware that its primary outsourcing provider occasionally used subcontractors to handle the daily processing of hundreds of files, it was unaware that the subcontractor used yet another subcontractor, who in turn offshored the work to a small work group in Pakistan. Even though the second and third outsource iterations were a breach of contract, the real problem occurred when the primary contractor paid the first subcontractor and that subcontractor paid the second subcontractor, but the second subcontractor did not pay the offshore provider. That offshore provider contacted UCSF Med Center via e-mail and threatened to post the medical records on the Internet if it was not paid the wages that were due.

The Med Center's problems began when the first outsourcing provider subcontracted work to a subcontractor, creating both contractual and integrity issues. A loosely monitored long-term agreement can lead to complacency, which can lead to stretching the boundaries of the agreement, which, in turn, can lead to trouble.

Organizations that are evaluating outsourcing on- or offshore must first question whether their vendors have integrity, and also question whether the vendors have a sufficiently vigorous security system. Service vendors must meet your security requirements, period.

This issue goes beyond an angry offshore vendor threatening to post personal data on the Internet; as banks, tax preparers, loan processors, medical records companies, and other organizations outsource (and offshore) sensitive materials, privacy concerns must be completely addressed. Organizations evaluating an outsourcing initiative need to ensure that their outsourced service vendors have suitably tough security practices that will meet the organization's internal requirements. The risk of security breaches or loss of intellectual property is amplified when working internationally, as legal systems in other countries may not offer the same intellectual property protection. Privacy concerns must be completely addressed; security requirements must be documented, monitored, and reported regularly; and the methods and integration with service vendors must be clearly defined.

Key point: Watch the valuables.

DELIVERY RISKS

A major issue facing organizations that choose to outsource involves delivery: the delivery of quality products or services, on time, within the scope of the contract, yet allowing for growth and innovation. If you have a great product with a great cost base, but your outsourcing vendor cannot get it to market on time, your outsourcing initiative is not working. If your vendor can get your product to market, but the product lacks quality, your customers will fill their product needs elsewhere, and your outsourcing initiative will fail.

Delivery issues—quality, growth, timing, and scope creep—must be addressed during the initial stages of your investigation. You must consider the following areas.

Delivery and Quality

Successful outsourcing is dependent on how well you define your customer requirements and how well you measure how those requirements are being met. If you cannot define or measure your requirements, you are doomed to fail. Delivery may be measuring call center turnaround time on responses to customer inquiries, and an added value (or additional quality) is the metric that keeps track of how many similar requests come in. On- or offshore, you must be specific and deliberate when documenting your expectations for delivery and quality.

Delivery and Growth

Your outsourcing vendor needs to be prepared to meet your growth requirements, so you must evaluate vendors' ability to ramp up when you need them. You must identify their ability to increase staff and skills to react to your needs.

Delivery and Deadlines

If your outsourcing vendor is unaware of, uninterested in, or unable to meet your delivery deadlines, you have a big problem, and big problems have big price tags. You must identify the vendor's sense of urgency by checking references, and, during the contract stage, you must set metrics to measure the vendor's observance of your timetables.

Delivery and Scope Creep

Fixed-price contracts just do not exist in outsourcing. Since outsourcing contracts contain baselines and assumptions, when the actual work varies from estimates, the organization will pay the difference. This risk has become a major difficulty for organizations that are surprised when the service vendor expects to be paid for incremental scope changes. Most projects change by 10 to 15 percent during the development cycle, so a vital part of due diligence is to get your hands around the scope of your project before you begin. Do your homework *at home* first, then do your homework outside.

> *Key point:* Assess delivery from every angle; validate your goals, objectives, and deliverables.

RISKS OF RULES AND REGULATIONS

Utilities, financial services institutions, drug companies, and health-care organizations, among others, face various degrees of government regulation. Noncompliance with government standards or insufficient "transparency" during an audit can spell big trouble. The issue of transparency is becoming more significant as requirements such as the Sarbanes-Oxley Act place greater burdens of accountability on all American corporations. Sarbanes-Oxley holds senior management accountable for the accuracy of financial statements; outsourcing financial activities requires great confidence in the service vendor's controls, abilities, and integrity. Outsourcing could make compliance more cumbersome and costly—and certainly more risky.

> *Key point:* Outsourcing does not minimize management's accountability; it intensifies management's accountability.

RISKS OF THE HUMAN ELEMENT

Unfortunately, organizations often underestimate the value of their employees, and therefore they also underestimate the impact of this human element on their overall outsourcing success. It is the people, after all, who actually get the job done—not processes, not tools, not specific sites or locations, just people. Successful outsourcing initiatives require seasoned professionals and dedicated workers in-house and off-site, and organizations are more likely to find those valuable candidates in their own backyard. Once you have excellent resources, keep them, invest in them, and value them, using communication as your platform.

Communication

One thing is certain: The world changes quickly, and most people change slowly. This slow-to-change tendency is aggravated when modifications are made to people's work processes, workplaces, or employment without their having an awareness, understanding, or input. A fearful and risk-averse employee base can be a very real danger to an organization, resulting in anything from turnover of key personnel to stress claims. To avoid and dispel fear, inform. To shift from risk aversion to support, inform. To let your employees know that you value them, inform.

People

Whether you outsource on- or offshore, you must strategize the process by which you will hire, train, reward, and maintain staff. In any outsourcing situation, there will be some level of attrition. If you do your homework, you will know what to expect; then you can create a process to manage it. If you do not want to risk losing all of the experience in your organization, you must make a plan to retain those you wish to keep.

When P&G planned to move from an internal solution to an outsourcing solution, approximately 7,000 employees were affected. At contract start-up, these P&G employees became employees of the outsourcing vendor. Because they were informed on an ongoing basis, these employees were aware of the process in front of them, as well as their value to the new organization; morale was high, and turnover was low.

If you must reduce staff to implement your outsourcing initiative, you must be aware of the potential for employee bitterness—demoralized employees do not feel valued and do not perform well. A well-rounded human resource strategy includes assisting your displaced employees to obtain additional training so that they can stay current in their field and providing some level of assistance in outplacement.

Key point: Retention of your best assets is critical—do not risk losing anyone because of a weak human resource strategy.

ADDITIONAL RISKS TO CONSIDER

In addition to the risks of quality, customer service, delivery, privacy and security, human resources, and compliance, outsourcing provides opportunities for additional—and very real—risks that you may not have considered.

Disaster Recovery

What happens if, for example, you outsource your call center to India, and it experiences a devastating earthquake? If you have an intelligent strategy to spread the risk, along with a sturdy disaster recovery plan, you will maintain a high customer satisfaction level while you dig out. If not, you risk losing just about everything.

In 2004, the U.S. government ordered flu vaccine from a source in the United Kingdom; that source found that the majority of its material was defective. The resulting shortage of flu vaccine was both tragic and avoidable; it is hard to ignore the fact that there was no alternative or backup plan and no additional resources from which to draw additional material. The government response to the shortage was to call on the public to "wash your hands more often."

A much more reliable and sensible process would have been to order vaccine from several sources, so that if a single source proved defective, the remaining sources could take up the slack.

Circle back now to the call center example in India. You must ask yourself: If my call center halfway around the world must close down because of some disaster, what is my plan? How long can we operate without a call center? How can we avoid the "wash your hands" reaction?

Political Concerns

There are additional geographical concerns when outsourcing offshore. A solid strategy must address the political stability of the location chosen, the possibility of civil strife, and potential political strains that might undermine your outsourcing project.

Legal Concerns

To ensure the success of your offshore initiative, you must visit the offshore site, and you must visit it often. How easy is it to travel to your offshore site, how often will you visit, and how difficult will it be to obtain visas? Labor laws, import and export licenses, tax implications, and customs issues all must be addressed and resolved.

Ethical Concerns

Running a domestic ethics program supported by employee training and a 1-800 hotline for reporting misconduct is thorny. Offshore, there are certain countries where there is an even higher risk for ethical breach because the pressure to pay bribes is greater. Global compliance with ethics programs is considerably more complex, and is hindered by cultural differences. On- or offshore, ethics must be addressed.

> *Key point:* Your due-diligence process must involve expertise beyond that of your outsourcing vendor.

THE REWARDS

Now for the good news, the rewards—and there are many.

IMPROVED BUSINESS FOCUS

Outsourcing allows companies to focus on their core skills and products as well as on more expansive business issues such as branding, strategy, and planning while having specific operational details handled by outside specialists. A company engaged in a well-calculated outsourcing initiative will benefit by focusing its resources on meeting the customer's needs, having been released from dedicating resources to areas outside of its business expertise. In addition to shifting the focus from peripheral activities toward work that is customer-facing, outsourcing can help managers set more specific priorities, and since their time and attention are not divided, they are able to deliver results.

REDUCED OR CONTROLLED OPERATING COST

Perhaps the single, most important tactical reason for outsourcing is the benefit of reducing and controlling operating costs. Gaining access to a vendor's lower cost structure is one of the most compelling short-term benefits of outsourcing.

Organizations that try to do everything themselves may actually experience elevated costs for research, development, marketing, and deployment expenses, and more; and all of these direct and indirect expenses are passed on to the consumer. Your outsourcing provider's reduced cost structure may be the result of greater economies of scale or other advantages based on specialization, and that reduced cost structure may increase your competitive advantage.

Cost cutting may not be, and should not be, the only reason to outsource, but it is undoubtedly a significant consideration. For most organizations, employee-related costs and the associated overhead expenses are relatively fixed, regardless of the demand for the organization's products or services, and during slow times this can be very expensive. Outsourcing allows you to convert fixed costs into variable costs, and your outsourcing provider can offer special pricing for this variable demand.

A recent study conducted by Accenture provides an overview of the fixed/variable-cost situation as it relates to airline companies. We know that airlines are in trouble around the globe, and we also know that they can use outsourcing to optimize their cost structures and achieve high performance.

With airline revenues down, with an oversupply of competitors, and with the vulnerabilities and uncertainties created by an unstable global economic and political landscape, it is no wonder that airlines all over the world are struggling to survive.

Airlines realize that they need cost management and efficiency strategies to improve their bottom lines and to compete with the successful business models of the low-cost/low-complexity airlines. The fundamental point of difference between the low-cost airlines and traditional airlines is the higher percentage of variable costs in their cost structure. Fixed costs make up 60 to 70 percent of the traditional network airline's costs; that is reduced to 50 to 60 percent at low-cost airlines.

Accenture recommends that airlines convert as many of their fixed costs as possible into variable costs, while lowering overall operating costs. This will allow them to be both flexible and efficient enough to prosper in slow or growing economies.

Accenture, using an outsourcing program designed to help airlines enhance the effectiveness of their cost structures and realign themselves for high performance, required an up-close concentration on outsourcing of noncore, rules-based, back-office functions and processes under a term contract to a specialist third party. Forward-thinking airlines are already outsourcing a wide range of noncore services such as finance and administration, information technology, and human resources, delivering significant cost savings to their organizations.

The airline industry is only one example of reducing costs through an outsourcing strategy. To save costs in any organization through outsourcing, make sure that your business model supports the need to outsource, investigate, test, and reap the rewards.

INCREASED ACCESS TO
WORLD-CLASS CAPABILITIES

By the very nature of their specialization, outsourcing providers bring extensive world-class resources to meet the needs of their customers. Partnering with an organization with outstanding capabilities can offer access to new technology, tools, and techniques that your organization may not currently possess. World-class providers make extensive investments in technology, methodologies, and people; they gain expertise by working with many clients who are facing similar challenges. This combination of specialization and expertise gives their customers a competitive advantage through these expanded skills, and helps them avoid the cost of chasing technology and training.

A LEVEL PLAYING FIELD

Most small companies simply cannot afford to match the in-house support services that larger companies maintain. Outsourcing can help smaller firms act "big" by giving them access to the same economies of scale, efficiency, and expertise that large companies enjoy.

According to the research group Gartner Inc. in Stamford, Connecticut, the small and midsize outsourcing market is growing 12 percent a year, and outsourcing vendors are rushing to grab a piece of this fast-growing market. Midsize organizations in particular stand to gain a lot from outsourcing; if it is done correctly, midsize organizations can maintain a smaller staff, and, as is the case with any size company, outsourcing noncore activities (for example, HR administration) can free up resources to focus on more strategic efforts.

RESOURCES REDIRECTED
TO MORE STRATEGIC ACTIVITIES

Every organization has limits on its available resources. Outsourcing allows resources to be redirected from non-core activities toward customer-facing activities that provide a greater return. Through a well-planned outsourcing initiative, your organization can redirect your displaced employees (or their head count) to greater value-adding activities.

CASH INFUSION

Outsourcing may involve the transfer of assets from the organization to the vendor or service provider. Equipment, facilities, vehicles, and licenses used in the current operations have value and are sold to the vendor. The vendor then uses these assets to provide services to the organization. Depending on the value of the assets involved, this sale may result in a significant cash payment to the organization. When these assets are sold to the vendor, they are typically sold at book value, which is often higher than market value. In these cases, the difference between the book value and market value may represent a loan from the vendor to the organization that is repaid in the price of the services over the life of the contract. In either event, the benefit of the potential cash infusion is undeniable, and the organization can use this cash infusion to redouble its customer-facing efforts, invest in retraining of displaced or transferred employees, or otherwise improve its business.

AVAILABILITY OF CAPITAL FUNDS

In most organizations, there is enormous competition for capital funds. Deciding where to invest these funds is one of the most crucial decisions for senior management; it is difficult for a senior manager to justify noncore capital investments over investments that are more directly related to the product, service, or customer.

Outsourcing reduces the need to invest capital funds in noncore business functions by contracting for these investments on an "as used" operational basis instead of acquiring the resources through capital expenditures. Outsourcing can also improve certain financial measures of the firm by eliminating the need to show a return on equity from capital investments in noncore areas.

CONCLUSIONS

The majority of problems with outsourcing deals are rooted in a deficient due-diligence process and poor communication. Executives who are considering an outsourcing program must clearly identify why they want to outsource and what they want to achieve through outsourcing, and they must carefully plan and execute a strong and extensive strategy in order to achieve a significant return on investment. Then, before commencing work with an outsourcing provider, executives must remember that making this process work requires building a relationship with the outsourcing provider; as in any relationship, communication and understanding of mutual expectations is critical to its development. There's a delicate balance between trusting your outsourcing provider and controlling your outsourcing provider, and striking that balance will help you develop and maintain a strong and long-term relationship.

Negotiating an outsourcing contract is never easy and can take years. While you are designing and developing a relationship that will last for five or more years, you are attempting to intuitively build in protections for both sides, while also attempting to predict any changes and mitigating any risks in an effort to benefit from the abundant rewards that can come about during that five-year time frame.

With strong leadership, proper planning, due diligence, and a well-built strategy, the benefits of an outsourcing program are plentiful. Risks are abundant (and certain) without these elements.

CHAPTER 4

DETERMINING WHAT TO OUTSOURCE

*It's not hard to make decisions
when you know what your values are.*

—ROY DISNEY

Since offshore outsourcing gained momentum on a foundation of information technology, many people assume that IT is the best or only business function to outsource. In actuality, while we know that many IT applications outsource well, including development maintenance/repair, reengineering, mainframe data enters, client/server networks, desktop systems, and end-user support, other functions outsource well, too. In fact, manufacturing, mortgage loan processing, back-office banking functions, customer care call centers, payroll, benefits management, tax compliance, and just about every other noncore function you can think of are candidates for outsourcing.

To fully understand the scope of possibilities and opportunities for outsourcing, I asked several experts and executives for their advice on identifying what to outsource and where. The experts included a manufacturing executive, a vice president of a prestigious research firm, a software executive, an IT consultant, and an attorney. Although they viewed the analysis and determination of what and where to outsource through differing filters, their advice provides a wealth of critical information on identifying functions to outsource based on the success factors of your organization (for example, cost, quality, and productivity), allowing you to rank those factors on the basis of their importance to your business. All of them agreed on three main factors:

1. You must identify and understand your values as they relate to your business.

2. You must never outsource a problem function.

3. If you are going to move a customer-facing service, you must involve your clients early.

THE IMPORTANCE OF A PROJECT MANAGER

Art Salyer, executive vice president of operations for Trojan Battery Company in California, has many years of successful outsourcing experience in manufacturing. He recommends that you begin your "what" analysis by pulling your leadership team together to discuss your present product processes and your initial expectations. Then, Salyer recommends appointing an initial project manager (PM) to take the executive team's recommendations to the next level. This PM's sole responsibility and focus is to initiate an assessment of your business functions or tasks for possible outsourcing. Remember, this PM may or may not be on your final outsourcing team—the skills that are needed at this time are objectivity, analysis, accuracy, and diplomacy. You could certainly hire a consultant at this point, but an outsourcing consultant has a vested interest in your ultimately outsourcing "everything," so it may be best to use an insider, or to hire a consultant with no ties to providers of outsourcing services.

One of the PM's first tasks is to conduct a readiness assessment of the organization to help determine exactly what kind of work should be outsourced. The assessment process will help you determine what skills you already have in-house, what skills are needed from a third-party source, and the cost implications of outsourcing. Using this information, you can then decide what the nature of the outsourcing relationship should be, and thus the type of vendor you need.

The PM is also responsible for communicating the goals of the outsourcing initiative directly to employees—they will find out what is happening one way or another, and it's best that they hear it from inside the organization. As decisions are made, staff may suffer from anxiety and uncertainty—typically, their "best" scenario is to have no change in their work or reporting structure; their "worst" scenarios range from being transferred to another employer to termination of their employment. Observe and respond to your staff's concerns during this process by offering as much information as possible, while also creating opportunities for question-and-answer sessions. Employees who are resistant to change will be more productive if they are included in the process.

It's also important for senior team members to show their support for the outsourcing initiative while providing existing employees with a constant flow of information; this type of support from upper management can be a big help when employees concerned about their future demonstrate any form of resistance to the plan.

Finally, and most importantly, the PM must develop a business plan that clearly explains the business drivers for the initiative and addresses the organization's readiness to manage the changes that will be required when the outsourcing initiative takes effect. If employees are to be laid off or retrained as a result of outsourcing, it's important to clearly communicate those plans early on. "You have to bring your people on board through clear communication strategies," Salyer said.

> *Key point:* Create a PM role for an internal leader with strong impartiality, investigative ability, preciseness, discretion, and diplomacy skills. If no one internally meets the full criteria, hire a consultant with no ties to outsourcing service providers.

THE DECISION TEAM

Linda Cohen, managing vice president of Gartner, Inc. in Connecticut, suggests that the PM create a core outsourcing team, or decision team, to further develop the outsourcing initiative. The purpose of this team is to decide what is in and what is out—and why. A sourcing strategy must be defined in business terms; the decision team must define the desired outcomes in business terms, must evaluate how internal staff can achieve those business goals, and then must define the outsourcing ROI to make sure that an outsourcing initiative is synchronized with business strategies.

The decision team is composed of executives, each of whom must offer support for the process in order for it to succeed. The decision team should include your human resource executive, CFO, CIO, legal counsel, governance executive, and business unit P&L owners. This group must be willing to do what is right for the company, even if that means outsourcing one of their own business units or deciding against the outsourcing initiative altogether. Objectivity may be difficult at this time, so the team members must be selected to have subject matter expertise as well as impartiality.

Key point: The decision team must treat this outsourcing initiative as an important project. The PM must be exclusive to this project, and the team must establish a method of working together, even though turf issues will arise, so that an effective action plan can be developed.

DEVELOP YOUR STRATEGY

Dr. Adam Kolawa, CEO of Parasoft, Inc. (a leading provider of automated error prevention software solutions across the globe) recommends that you begin your "what" analysis with one fundamental question: What are the things I don't need to do myself? Discovering what to outsource, and where, takes strategy, and Dr. Kolawa advises executives to consider his three-step approach to identifying what should be outsourced:

1. DETERMINE THE MAIN FOCUS OF YOUR COMPANY

Why are you in business? What are you trying to accomplish, and what do your customers see as your unique value? Once you identify your main event, or the primary competitive advantage of your organization, you can clearly articulate your goals and center your energies—and the energy of your team—on any projects that are directly related to that main focus. The only projects to be considered for outsourcing are those that are not directly related to your main event.

2. ANALYZE YOUR COMPANY

Is this a task, product, or service that you really need to build or provide in-house? Is it unique or complicated?

It is important to take a critical look at the resources in your company. If you ask engineers whether they can build a certain part, they always answer "yes." That's how we engineers are—a better question is, "Why is this part critical to my business?" In other words, we must ask if we have enough knowledge in-house to do this more effectively than anyone else.

If not, Kolawa says, "It is not important to your company, and is a good candidate for outsourcing."

With your main event in mind, you can begin to concentrate the efforts of your team on becoming better in the specialty of your business. Those projects that are not essential to your main event can, if placed in the right hands, potentially reduce costs, improve quality, and increase production.

3. BUILD RELATIONSHIPS WITH VENDORS THAT SPECIALIZE

First, the relationship part of the equation: The primary means of creating stability in your outsourcing program is to develop a long-term relationship with your outsourcing vendors. Developing an outsourcing program based on a short-term goal of saving money, without strong vendor relationships, often leads to quick but temporary cost savings. With due diligence, you can build relationships with your vendors and experience long-term rewards.

Now for the specialization part of the equation: Those projects that are not essential to your main event can provide significant rewards if outsourced. Dr. Kolawa recommends that you let outsourcing vendors that specialize concentrate their efforts for you. (See Chapter 5 for additional information on vendor selection and specialization.)

> *Key point:* Conduct a thorough review of all organizational processes. This review will enable you to maintain a clear vision of your direction while eliminating the possibility of outsourcing a function or process that may be better integrated with one of your main event functions.

WATCH THE
CUSTOMER-FACING ACTIVITIES

Phillip Hatch, president of Ventoro.com, likes to begin working with organizations considering an outsourcing solution early.

> We like to have customers bring us in at the beginning. That way, we can help them cut the nonsense and help them build a business case for the best answer for them. We begin by quantifying the problem, for example, reducing costs. We recommend they talk with their customers, talk with their shareholders, any other stakeholders, and their employees to make sure they all see the problem in the same way, so they can begin to research possible solutions. Without that, you are doomed to fail.

For example, Hatch relates a situation with a major high-tech client who wrote a blanket policy: We will move everything to India. There was no understanding of why, there were no benefits outlines, the senior team did not all agree or support the strategy, and consequently there were no real benefits.

Most of all, talk with your customers. There are some client-specific issues that must be addressed before engaging in an outsourcing situation. A client recently engaged us to help them with an outsourcing problem they encountered. They had selected, with the help of an outsourcing consultant, an offshore solution to reduce the costs of their residential refinance call center. Prior to the outsourcing to India, the call center was in California, and the call center reps handled refinance questions and made cold calls to their Spanish-speaking customer base. The organization closed the California call center, fired all the employees, offshored the work, and only then found out there were no Spanish-speaking call centers in India.

Hatch related another example of a customer-facing process that should not have been outsourced involving a high-end software company in Tennessee. This company creates intricate systems for finance companies like Citigroup, Mellon Financial, and Deutsche Bank—with typical transactions between $10 and $50 million. Before outsourcing, when the software company signed a new client, the software rep would provide high-touch, personalized care for the client. They were dealing with people at the executive vice president and senior vice president level, and whenever there was a question or an issue, the software rep would hop on a plane and walk the client through the fix.

This created a solid experience for the client, a warm interface that allowed a high level of trust to exist.

The software company wanted to reduce the cost of its customer service, so, without informing its clients, it removed the 24-hour domestic response team and moved it to India. When the problem calls from the executive and senior vice presidents came in, those executives were expecting that high-touch response (hop on a plane and help me), and that response was not available from the new service vendor in India.

> *Key point:* Before you outsource or offshore any customer-facing process or service, you need to know how your customers feel about it.

DETERMINE YOUR
OUTSOURCING OPPORTUNITIES

George Spafford, an experienced IT practitioner and founder of Spafford Consulting, recommends that you create a list of every activity your business performs. This could include

- Accounts payable/receivable

- Application development and maintenance

- Asset management

- Benefits administration

- Equipment support, maintenance, and other cross-functional services

- Financial management, analysis, and reporting

- General accounting

- Help desk functions

- Information technology and telecommunications

- Intranet and Internet support and hosting

- Logistics and distribution

- Mailroom and administration

- Order taking/order fulfillment

- Payroll

- Relocation

- Repairs, returns processing

- Research

- Tax consulting and compliance

Consider every business activity carried out by one of your employees. Then consider these activities from your customer's point of view: Which of them are directly or indirectly related to your customer's decision to purchase your products or services, and to continue to purchase your products and services? Place those functions or tasks that may interfere with your customers in Quadrant 1 on the matrix in Figure 4.1.

Next, consider how well you perform the remaining activities from a qualitative and cost-effectiveness perspective. Separate those activities that you perform expertly from those activities that are mediocre and those that are not functioning well. Add all expert and mediocre functions to the grid in Quadrants 3 and 4; put the broken functions in Quadrant 2.

• *Quadrant 1 (top left)*. Customer-facing or other main event functions that must stay in-house.

• *Quadrant 2 (top right)*. Functions that are failing or broken, and thus are not candidates for outsourcing at this time.

• *Quadrant 3 (bottom left)*. Functions that are not directly related to your main event that you do well (in terms of productivity, quality, and cost).

• *Quadrant 4 (bottom right)*. Functions that are not directly related to your main event that are less than successful, but not broken.

Quadrant 1 Activities that interfere with customer purchase decision; must stay in-house	**Quadrant 2** Failing or broken processes or activities
Quadrant 3 Healthy noncore business activities; good candidates for outsourcing	**Quadrant 4** Adequate (but not broken) noncore business activities, could be enhanced through outsourcing

Figure 4.1

Before moving forward, identify and understand the many levels of business activities that your organization performs, and develop a strategy to outsource only those for which this will improve your business in some way.

Key point: Determining what to outsource is the decision team's main goal. By focusing on the core competencies of the organization, you are focusing on your uniqueness in the marketplace. The functions outside of your core are potential targets for outsourcing.

PROCESS REVIEW

Brad Peterson is an attorney and a partner in Mayer, Brown, Rowe & Maw, the leading legal resource for everything outsourced. Peterson recommends that the decision team review the following types of due diligence commonly conducted in an outsourcing transaction:

- Once proper communications with employees concerning the possibility of an outsourcing initiative are made, interview or survey the people currently performing the processes (including customers and third-party personnel).

- Review any written documentation of the in-scope processes, including any reports or data that identify current performance and quality levels.

- Identify performance, quality, and cost-improvement opportunities.

- Document your relevant findings in a form suitable to become a schedule to your outsourcing agreement.

When your team has reviewed your grid, addressed Quadrant 2 issues, and objectively measured the rewards of outsourcing the selected functions against the status quo, you are ready to move on to vendor selection.

OVERVIEW: BASIC DON'TS AND DO'S

DON'TS

- Don't outsource a broken process or function, ever.

- Don't let potential cost savings be your main decision driver.

- Don't be swayed by outsourcing consultants whose main purpose is to get you to outsource everything to one of their subsidiaries; your decision team must be objective.

- Don't outsource any decision making.

- Don't rush. Each function you decide to outsource may involve a long-term contract. Be methodical in your business planning before moving on to selecting an outsourcing vendor.

DO'S

- Let your PM focus solely on this project. It cannot be done well on a part-time basis.

- Work with your decision team to clarify your vision of your desired outcomes.

- When you determine what to outsource, be certain to outsource only the performance of the function, not the responsibility for the function.

- Benchmark your performance on the functions you are considering for outsourcing, and use this as a basis for comparison during vendor selection.

- Do your homework.

- Think it through.

- Take your time.

Now you are ready to begin the vendor selection process.

CHAPTER 5

CRITICAL SUCCESS FACTORS IN VENDOR SELECTION

In order to create early and sustainable growth through outsourcing, you must pick a vendor or service vendor who knows what to do, how to do it, how well to do it, and how quickly to do it. A complex process at best, vendor selection involves defining detailed business requirements, developing a business model and delivery model, developing an RFI (request for information) or RFP (request for proposal) document, evaluating and selecting vendors, conducting due diligence, including management interviews and site visits, finalizing the operating model, creating the governance structure, and finally negotiating the contract and SLA (service-level agreement).

To help you wade through this multistep process more effectively, our experts and executives offered advice in several critical areas—and they all agreed on two critical issues:

1. Take your time. Do not rush to meet a vendor's need to complete the transaction.

2. Do your homework.

Exploratory conversations can provide the foundation for a good match if all parties are candid about the factors that are crucial to a successful outsourcing relationship.

WHERE TO BEGIN

Binod Taterway is a principal partner in Blue Canopy, a leading business and IT consultancy whose clients include Marriott, UPS, AT&T, and AOL. Taterway developed what Blue Canopy calls the 4pi (or fourth-party integrator) methodology to help CIOs manage their multisource environments (MSE) more effectively throughout the entire life cycle of sourcing, including strategy, organizational readiness, implementation, transition, and governance.

Taterway suggests that one underlying problem in outsourcing is that organizations are not process-driven. Outsourcing forces process on organizations: "You can't be ad hoc from 10,000 miles away. Organizations who do not think and operate by process before they outsource or offshore will fail miserably."

Many IT outsourcing consultants focus on getting the best deal from their client's vendors or service providers—and the best "deal" is often based on price alone, which "seldom works over a long period of time," Taterway explains. "IT service vendors need to become an integral part of the service supply chain."

Taterway recommends that organizations focus on these key challenges when they evaluate outsourcing vendors:

• *Maturity.* Is your organization ready in terms of the infrastructure needed to manage the process? "Most organizations still operate in functional silos that will create problems when it comes to managing outsourcing service providers."

- *Benefits.* What, exactly, are the benefits you expect to achieve? Having a strategic business case "sets the economic expectations of outsourcing."

- *Proof of concept.* This process of testing moves from pencil proof to tangible proof of concept, which is recommended before embarking on any outsourcing deal.

- *Sponsorship.* Does the entire management team buy into this initiative? Without support throughout the organization, all the way to the top, you are setting yourself up for failure.

- *Investment.* Do you have the financial support to manage external service providers?

- *Governance.* Will your prospective vendor work with you to develop a set of rules that define roles and responsibilities, rights, and principles, accountabilities and procedures, along with an escalation process that guides decision making, problem resolution, and ongoing changes in the outsourcing engagement? As your team works to select the best outsourcing option, time should be spent in discussions with prospective vendors to define a governance model that is clear and thorough enough to avoid uncertainty, while still being flexible enough to enable quick changes that may be required during the course of your contract. The focus of your governance model will include the identification of roles and responsibilities, rights, and accountabilities for both parties, along with principles that will guide decisions, a method for escalating when necessary, and specific guidelines and procedures for dealing with changes or problems.

"To a large extent," Taterway explains, "most organizations do not know exactly how to do outsourcing. It is not like a purchase from a supermarket: Buy it and I am done." The process of developing a successful outsourcing initiative is customized and evolutionary; the one-size-fits-all approach to outsourcing does not work. Taterway recommends that organizations learn as much about outsourcing as possible before beginning the search for vendors. The advantages your organization may reap from outsourcing will vary with the services outsourced, your business model, and the quality of your vendor, and it is essential that you move slowly and methodically through this process.

Once you have completed the basic information-gathering process, it is time to pull together a group of people who understand the need, support the outsourcing vision, and are ready to take the time to conduct in-depth research to select the right service provider.

THE VENDOR SELECTION TEAM

Linda Cohen, our expert from Gartner, Inc., recommends that a new outsourcing team be convened: a vendor selection team. The primary purpose of this group is to shop for vendors and to develop the metrics to be used during the transition and afterward—the "make it work" team. This team, an operational management committee from various parts of operations, should include internal clients of the service (those internal people who are currently receiving the service to be outsourced) and individuals who are currently responsible for providing the service (those who will give up the service to the outsourcing provider). The skills required of these team members include the following:

- *Objectivity and tenacity.* The ability to maintain a level of impartiality, while staying with the task through what might be uncomfortable decisions, in an effort to provide a meaningful result to the organization

- *Strong analytical abilities.* The ability to consider apples and oranges and compare the unique benefits of sometimes conflicting information

- *Good listening skills.* The ability to listen carefully to allow for better understanding of issues, assignments, and expectations

- *Variety orientation.* The ability to work in an environment with tough problems and fast-paced change

- *Patience.*

"The vendor selection team (VST) will be guided by the information and research provided by the decision team," continues Cohen.

The "why are we doing this" question has been fully answered, the benchmarks have been set, and the due-diligence process now begins to identify vendors with a better, faster, cheaper way of providing this service. With a strong and supportive committee overseeing the vendor selection, your organization can create a sourcing strategy that is defined in business terms: understanding how internal staff currently achieve their business goals, then defining your desired outcomes to make sure your sourcing selection corresponds with your business strategies. Your VST is responsible for developing and articulating expectations in terms of ROI (return on investment), for selecting the delivery model that will get you where you want to be, and for creating the balance of trust and control that will be the foundation for a long and rewarding relationship.

A BEST PRACTICE
IN OUTSOURCING PLANNING

George Spafford recommends that organizations, when talking with outside consultants, first evaluate those consultants' focus. Do they understand what is needed? Do they have their own agenda? Are they overly broad or too narrow? Are they aiming to create a real solution for you, or simply to create a straw house that will require years of additional support, "with an increase in the associated fees"?

According to Spafford, "A series of controls can be implanted in such a way as to create a framework. Within the framework, the people, the processes, and the technology are integrated to protect what matters most to the organization."

Some vendors, especially those that are tied to manufacturing plants or service delivery companies overseas, may try to force their version of a control framework onto your organization without specifically customizing it to fit you. "You absolutely need to have a control framework that is tailored to your organization's needs," says Spafford.

This means you must have the right people following the right process for the right reasons. You never want to say, "We do it this way because our consultant told us so"—understand what is vital to your organization, what must be done to protect it, and maintain the decision making in-house.

The three main keys for success here are having the right people internally supporting the project, working from a specific and comprehensive requirements definition, and diligently and proactively practicing risk management to find the right solution for your organization through the right source. Then your internal team can work with the structure you've created—don't be pushed by a vendor."

THE RIGHT SOURCE

Brad Peterson, an attorney and a partner in Mayer, Brown, Rowe & Maw, states, "Effective relationships rely on having the right match of customer and vendor. If the customer and vendor are well matched, many of the other issues can simply be negotiated." In an effort to create value in an outsourcing transaction, Peterson offers selection criteria for review during the vendor selection process: The vendor's delivery capability, track record, and reputation; and the relationship between your needs and the vendor's capacity in terms of scale, commitment to training, and continuous improvement need to be reviewed. In more detail, a good due diligence process also includes

- A compatible corporate culture, whether informal or formal in style, in terms of centralized or decentralized management; the conflict resolution process; flexibility; process, idea, people, or action orientation; business tactics; information flow; perception of reasonableness and risks; meaning attached to commitments; long-term versus short-term orientation; customer, engineering, or market focus; and so on

- The vendor's delivery capability in the function to be outsourced and related areas

- The vendor's track record in the market or industry, or with the customer

- The match between the customer's needs and the vendor's capabilities in terms of geography and scale

- Opportunities to expand the scope of your project

- Conflicts of interest (Peterson asks, "Does one party serve the other party's competitors? Do the parties or their close allies compete directly?")

- Existence of appropriate capabilities and interests in the vendor's subcontractors and alliance partners

- The vendor's commitment to training, research, development, and continuous improvement

- Price

- Trust

Developing a good working relationship is a balance of trust, predictability, and control. "You want to treat your outsourcing vendors as strategic rather than tactical," Peterson says. "Use a collaborative approach, including parties working to achieve the promised benefits and each party seeking ways to make both parties more successful."

A SYSTEMATIC APPROACH
TO VENDOR SELECTION

The outsourcing industry is segmented in a number of different ways, so before you begin your systematic approach to vendor selection, you must have a clear understanding of your specific needs and the type of provider that can best meet them. To start a search, network within your industry for referrals, read trade publications (reports rather than advertisements), use the Internet, or engage a consultant (with no ties to a specific provider) to assist in the research.

Phillip Hatch of Ventoro.com recommends that organizations begin the vendor selection process by first locating all vendors with the specific industry expertise and technical skills. The research can be accomplished in-house through your VST, Hatch says,

> But you must find these vendors, regardless of their country, and you must not be persuaded by vendors or consultants claiming that a lack of industry expertise or technical skills is not an issue.
>
> Once you have a comprehensive list of all vendors with the appropriate industry and technical skills, issue an RFI to communicate your business needs, and let the vendors respond with their potential solution. We recommend you do not include your potential solution in your RFI, but that you use the process as an opportunity to see how each vendor would approach and respond to your needs.

Hatch recommends that the VST read and weigh each RFI response carefully and filter out those firms that you do not believe have taken the RFI process seriously and those that fail to offer any insight into how they would approach your specific problem. "If a vendor lacks interest and responsiveness at this point in the process, you know exactly what you can expect after the contract is signed," Hatch says.

"Once you have filtered out the pretenders," Hatch advises, "issue an RFP asking for bids on a well-defined implementation." The RFP document must be prepared as clearly as possible to prevent any ambiguity in the final analysis process. Your RFP must ask questions specific to a vendor's capability to provide you with the services you need, for example,

- Include a comprehensive description of your expectations for the relationship, and ask the vendor how it intends to fulfill these expectations.

- Ask for information on the vendor's management capability, relationship management, reporting, and policy or procedural compliance.

- Ask for training requirements for new employees and the amount of recurring training needed to maintain proficiency. Ask for turnover reports, and ask how the training program will help achieve a balanced and qualified workforce.

- State your quality monitoring and reporting requirements. Ask if all of the elements required (equipment, human resources, and processes) are present in the vendor's current program.

- Describe success, including a full complement of requirements necessary to achieve the successful results you wish to attain.

- Request pricing, including start-up, training, and reporting costs and any other fees that might be associated with the project. By breaking down each cost on a line-item basis, you can better compare vendors in the final stages of your selection process.

• Timetable: Request the vendor's transition plan, timing, and key personnel responsible for working directly with your staff to implement the outsourcing initiative.

Your VST must carefully review these proposals by conducting an aggressive research campaign for each vendor, including:

1. For each vendor, find its current and excustomers, independent of the references that the vendor's sales team has provided. Pay particular attention to

   • The vendor's ability to execute against the plan

   • The vendor's integrity

   • The vendor's level of professionalism

   • The vendor's ability to solve problems

   • The vendor's flexibility

   • The vendor's financial strength and stability

   • The vendor's "customer-centric" level

2. Once the independent study has been completed, follow up on the remaining issues within the RFP, including

   • The vendor's references and reputation as provided by the sales team—do they agree or disagree with the references and reputation you found previously?

   • The vendor's flexibility on contract terms—how do these flexibility issues compare and contrast with your independent research?

   • The vendor's financial strength, again measured against your real-time research.

   • Price—a consideration purposely placed at the bottom of the list. If the other issues are unclear or unacceptable, no amount of special pricing will make the relationship worth the trouble.

3. In many RFPs, the vendor will identify key resources—people—to be assigned to your outsourcing process. While turnover can be quite high, the opportunity to read résumés and interview these key people is valuable. At the very least, ensure that

- The people actually exist.
- Each individual is a current employee of the vendor.
- The experience levels match the résumés.
- The academic and professional credentials are legitimate.
- The behavioral style of your key contacts is compatible with that of the individual managing the process in-house (see Chapter 7 for more information on building a team that works).

4. For those gold standard vendors that you are seriously considering, conduct a site visit, touring their major fulfillment locations. This will allow you to determine whether the facilities match the description given by the sales team in the RFP, observe whether the employees working in these facilities are motivated and professional, and give you an idea of what elements of the vendor's recommendations you can live without.

5. Weighing both the hard and soft issues of vendor selection is made easier with a vendor-selection checklist. Use Table 5.1 as a template to the critical issues and weight them for your company. If you are outsourcing offshore, you may want to add questions on culture,

Table 5.1 Vendor-Selection Checklist

Question	Parameters	Weight	Vendor 1	Vendor 2
1	*Experience and expertise.* How long has this vendor been in this business, and what similar project experience does this vendor have?	0.15		
2	*Track record, part 1.* Past performance, customer focus, and reputation *as disclosed by sales staff.*	0.02		
3	*Track record, part 2.* Past performance, customer focus, and reputation as disclosed *through independent research.**	0.07		
4	*Site visit.* Do the facilities meet your requirements?	0.1		
5	*Financial strength.* Do the vendor's financial standing, creditworthiness, and stability support the significant investment you will make, or is it a start-up or thinly capitalized?	0.1		
6	*Flexibility.* Business model, contract, and scalability.	0.15		
7	*Integrity.* Confidentiality, security, intellectual property rights norms, business model, quality standards.	0.17		
8	*People.* Real, active employees; legitimate education and certifications.	0.17		
9	*Price and margin.*	0.15		

* If there is a difference between the independent research and the references provided by the vendor, alter your scores accordingly.

language, additional security/privacy, legal issues, and governance.

"Once you have completed your research," Hatch says,

We recommend performing a limited pilot with the top two firms you have selected. This pilot should be three to six months in length, and should be significant enough to push both your firm and the vendor, while not opening up your organization to any additional risk. At the conclusion of the pilot, choose the best performing vendor for your long-term projects.

THE EXECUTIVE'S EXPERIENCE

Dick LeFave is senior vice president and chief information officer for Nextel Communications in Reston, Virginia. He has responsibility for the strategic deployment of information technology (IT) resources throughout Nextel, and with over 30 years' experience in the field of IT and management, he is no stranger to outsourcing. "Every time you do one, you learn something new. The first question we asked was, 'Why do it?' You have to be so very clear in your mind about what makes sense here: Is it money, skills, to be more effective, all of the above?"

After asking why, LeFave asked, "Do we know what 'it' is that we're looking for?" One of the major reasons it made sense to Nextel, a company that was growing quickly, was its need to generate scale.

It made sense for us because internally we could not scale fast enough. We pulled a good team of people together—supply chain, finance, tech, and IT—and we relied on an outside consultant to give us good strong structure to establish a methodology. With their help, our team developed good benchmark data, evaluations, templates that made the process efficient.

Before you sign any contract, build a financial model of what it takes to do it yourself. Then think like the vendor—they will figure out a way to save money, and if they can, why can't you? If they have a bigger scale, go for it. We looked at predictability of service level—the budget, unit costs, and the ability to add more services, storage, and people—versus do I have my own capacity model to accomplish the same things?

LeFave believes that the keys to success are modeling and the business case. The process must withstand the test of time – LeFave holds monthly "true-ups" to balance the trust/control issue.

We hold quarterly senior management meetings to maintain support and awareness, and we listen to the stories. Billions of dollars, lots of delivery, and when these deals go bad, they can take a lot with them. We stay on top of it, and we review the business case once per year, asking again, "why did we do this?" and true it up against the original benefit model. It's all about value.

CONCLUSION

The vendor selection process is not for the faint of heart, for organizations in a hurry, or for organizations that lack complete internal support. Done well, the process will be remarkably slow, yet it is that deliberate, unhurried approach that leads to outsourcing success.

The rewards of outsourcing are available to those who give their VST the time, resources, and authority to make the right decisions.

CHAPTER 6

TRANSITION BLUEPRINT

Most experts agree that the transition period—that is, the period between vendor selection and beginning operations with your new vendor—is critical. The transition period is known to be the most expensive stage of an outsourcing process, and it may take from three months to a full year to completely hand the work over to a new vendor or partner. Executives, be warned: There will be no cost savings, but rather significant expenses, during this period.

To make the transition process swift (not rushed) and effective, the following elements must be taken into consideration:

- *Strategy.* Prepare a comprehensive overview of your plan, especially as it relates to the remaining in-house business units.

- *Change management.* Create and implement a communication plan to inform and include employees; know the signs of resistance, and be prepared to deal directly with them.

- *Activities.* Identify and articulate the levels of service your organization actually needs in order to function.

- *Timeline.* Determine how swiftly, or how gradually, the transition will be implemented; integrate your entire transition plan into your agreement for service.

- *Financial plan.* Determine price, scope (and scope creep), and flexibility.

- *Resources.* Create a method by which the level of human capital is preserved or enhanced.

Beginning with the end in mind, develop your transition plan using these six elements, and the advice of our experts.

A WORD ABOUT STRATEGY

Creating your transition strategy is no different from developing a marketing strategy, a sales strategy, or a career strategy. A typical strategy begins with the identification of the starting point, and then focuses on the desired results, the alignment of resources, and finally the execution of the plan. Organizations that empower their management team to achieve the predetermined desired outcomes; those that monitor, measure, report, and review the activities of the vendor; and those that emphasize people development, both in-house and outsourced, are the most successful; problems ensue when organizations move from their starting point to the plan execution without concentrating on the results and resources.

The starting point and desired outcomes for your organization have been determined through your due-diligence and vendor identification process. The remaining strategy elements, alignment of resources and execution of the plan (including the monitoring process), must be determined and followed closely. Use your strategy to assist in the creation of a business model that works for your current and future needs, while coordinating and integrating with your entire organization.

THE VENDOR SELECTION TEAM AS THE TRANSITION TEAM

Linda Cohen, managing vice president of Gartner, Inc., recommends that the vendor selection team work through the transition plan in terms of strategy, timing, activities, budget, and resources, including what you will use to measure the success or failure of the process. Collaborating with your new vendor (not being *driven* by your new vendor) will allow you to make choices that best suit your business and financial goals. While you don't want to tell your outsourcing provider how to carry on its business, you do want to work with your provider's best practices to bring the cost savings in over time. "For example," Cohen said, "If I hire someone to clean my house and I insist that they use my tools and my products, I am simply hiring labor. I will not be exposed to any new tools or products, or any additional sources of process improvement." Work with your new service provider to develop a system that works for your organization, while focusing on innovations in process or technology that will make your cost to operate even lower.

Once the transition plan is complete, Cohen recommends developing an ongoing operations management team, or OMT.

These are the people remaining on staff charged with managing the outcome. The old-world in-sourced manager should not manage the vendor—typically, the in-sourced managers are process managers, focusing on the *how*. There is a different set of metrics needed here, because the focus is no longer on how work is performed, but rather on the expected outcome, or the *what*. It is hard for current staff, because they have always managed the how rather than the what.

MANAGING CHANGE

One of the most complex issues of good leadership is developing an environment in which change is encouraged, accepted, and managed. Managers and executives often report that their subordinates and colleagues resist change, and when planning and implementing an outsourcing strategy, alleviating the resistance to change is a daily necessity.

The easy answer to the resistance dilemma is to advise, inform, and communicate with your staff. However, to develop a best practice in communicating, you must understand the three basic stages of resistance: status quo, OK if, and finally commitment.

STATUS QUO

A popular behavioral assessment called DISC is a tool that creates an overview of an individual's behavioral preferences in four categories: D for Dominance, or how you deal with problems and challenges, I for Influence, or how you deal with people, S for Steadiness or how you deal with risk and change, and C for Compliance, or how you deal with procedures and rules. According to DISC assessment research, over 40 percent of the population prefer to have their world—at work and at home—clearly defined and predictable, without any unknown factors that might alter their ability to meet the specific requirements of their job. People with this behavioral style are consistent, dependable, and stable, and they tend to resist change until they completely understand how it will affect or disrupt their world.

This status quo approach to change may apply to all DISC styles, and is often not immediately obvious as the signs of resistance may be subtle; forgetting to attend a meeting about a proposed change or arriving for work late during transitional stages are symptoms of resistance that are often seen in people with the status quo approach. You may notice increased anger or disagreements, or perhaps withdrawal from participation within the team. Individuals may feel that they have not been involved in the change planning, and that while they have given their best at work, they are uncertain that they will survive the coming changes.

Productivity plummets during this stage, while sickness, accidents, and missed work increase. The status quo stage is the most disruptive; without proper involvement and communication, those employees who are resistant to change will most likely dust off their résumés and prepare to move to what they perceive to be a more stable workplace. At this stage, employees are laden with fear, uncertainty, and doubt (FUD), which are exacerbated when news of an impending outsourcing initiative is delivered via the rumor mill.

OK, IF

This stage of resistance is demonstrated by individuals saying, "OK, I'll try it, and once I see that it works . . ." During this stage, the resistant employee is seeking a guarantee that the risk or change that is on the table will be successful, allowing him or her to define the new boundaries of the change before actually committing to it. The key here is to involve, inform, and communicate so that the resistant employee understands the risks associated with the outsourcing initiative, good or bad, and can move away from the indecision platform and move on to commitment.

COMMITMENT

When employees have learned from the executive team about an upcoming outsourcing initiative and have been allowed to participate in some of the decisions, you will begin to hear, "When will I be trained on this?" or "How can I help make this a smooth transition?" The commitment stage is evident when employees demonstrate energy about the change and speak with optimism about the outcome.

Dr. Larry Ponemon, our ethicist, agrees that, internally, each organization will face ethical consequences if it implements before planning. Before making the transition, before signing a contract, Ponemon urges organizations to consider the ethical implications of the transition, including employees becoming withdrawn, engaging in nefarious activities, producing poor work results, and just plain slacking off.

Ponemon related an anonymous case study in which an organization announced to its employees that an offshore outsourcing program would be implemented over the course of the following three or four months. Once the outsourcing contract was signed, the organization announced that the new offshore employees would be flown in from India, and that the in-house, but soon to be displaced, onshore employees would be responsible for providing process training to their replacements. The new offshore employees were deliberately trained incorrectly by the old-world employees, including on such issues as privacy policy, which left the organization open to class action suits.

Prepare for the ethical pressures that will surely come as a result of your transition by communication and valuing your employees.

> "Communications to staff can always be better."
> DICK LEFAVE, CIO OF NEXTEL

OVERCOMING THE RESISTANCE TO CHANGE

Dick LeFave, CIO of Nextel, argues that an organization can "never overcommunicate." A well-designed communication plan will move people through the natural resistance stages into the commitment stage more quickly. Executives and experts agree that open and honest communication lessens employees' fear and increases their acceptance, yet many organizations, fearful that informed employees are more apt to leave, often make the mistake of decreasing their employee communications during an outsourcing initiative. The result is often a mass exodus of the very employees the organization would like to retain.

A strong, broad, and frequent communications plan must be incorporated into your overall outsourcing strategy. Work with your new outsourcing vendor to develop Web pages, all-hands meetings, newsletters, or intranet e-mail to communicate with your employees. Recruit supportive leaders throughout the organization to help educate others, while boosting their confidence in a process that may appear ambivalent, especially in the early stages. Get the word out on a regular basis so that your more resistant staff members can more clearly understand and participate in the changes ahead.

Phillip Hatch, president of Ventoro.com, recommends that executives add certainty and assurance to all of their commutations with staff.

The process of defining and implementing an out-sourcing strategy is an incredibly threatening proposition to your in-house team, and although you may have clearly articulated that there is no cause for fear, your in-house team will continue to be extremely edgy for some time to come. In our research we found this uncertainty among in-house teams does have a material impact on the overall success of the outsourcing strategy, requiring aggressive steps be taken to ease the concerns.

In order to swiftly move your most valuable resources, your employees, to embrace the outsource initiative, Hatch recommends taking several steps.

1. CLEARLY EXPLAIN YOUR PLANS

Throughout the entire outsourcing research and implementation process (and for some time after launch), meet frequently with your in-house team and present your master plan. Take the time to explain the specific objectives that the team must accomplish, how each person in the team will fit into the long-term plan, and what you expect from each team member in accomplishing each goal.

2. DEFINE CAREER GROWTH OPPORTUNITIES

Meet with employees individually prior to implementation of the outsourcing strategy to establish a clear plan for each individual to succeed. As soon as you announce plans to implement an outsourcing initiative, begin scheduling these meetings.

3. LET EMPLOYEES KNOW THAT THEY ARE VALUABLE

On a regular basis, let team members know just how important they are to both your organizational goals and the success of the outsourcing strategy.

4. NO BALONEY

Most important: do not try to con your way though the outsourcing strategy with your employees. Your in-house team knows your business well, and if you

- Outsource without a strong business case

- Misrepresent the business case

- Misrepresent the in-house employees' role in the outsourcing strategy

your team will know, and your team *will leave*. Even if you do plan to reduce head count, you need the support of the remaining team to accomplish your goals, and that support is tied directly to your integrity and credibility. Be very clear on what actions are being taken and why, and include your team as much as possible.

MANAGING THE ACTIVITIES, TIMELINES, BUDGET, AND RESOURCES

The disparity in expectations between vendor and organization is often the basis for outsourcing failure. To alleviate the differences in expectations, the VST must develop a comprehensive service-level agreement (SLA) as an integral part of your overall vendor contract.

Although an SLA is an excellent tool for managing mutual expectations, it is also valuable for enabling both the vendor and the organization to manage their own responsibilities and accountabilities. A strong SLA can be

- Another method by which the organization and the vendor open communications with each other and with the staff

- A conflict prevention tool, averting disputes by providing a shared understanding of the needs and priorities of all parties

- A dynamic document—an SLA can be reviewed on a predetermined schedule to assess service delivery and negotiate adjustments

- An objective yardstick for measuring service effectiveness, as both parties will use the same criteria to evaluate quality

To be effective, an SLA must incorporate two sets of elements: service elements and management elements. The service elements portion identifies the requirements definitions by communicating such things as

- Services provided, and perhaps a list of certain services not provided, especially if the organization might reasonably expect such services to be available

- Conditions of service availability

- Service standards, including timelines and time frames within which services will be provided

- Mutual responsibilities for transition and delivery

- Cost versus service negotiations

- Escalation procedures

The management elements of a good SLA concentrate on such things as

- How service effectiveness will be monitored and tracked, by whom, and how often

- How information about service effectiveness will be reported and addressed

- How service-related disagreements will be resolved

- How each party will review and revise the agreement

Planning a successful outsourcing experience requires a comprehensive SLA, far beyond simply plugging service elements into a typical template. Before beginning your SLA effort, work with your VST to ensure that you have the knowledge and skill base to proceed; if you find that your team is deficient in some capacity, identify a resource to fill the spot. Your VST, along with your attorney, vendor, and customers, may spend several months gathering, examining, documenting, and presenting information before negotiating, and finally agreeing on a process and components that will work.

> "The biggest problem I've seen in outsourcing is that U.S. companies aren't big on requirements definitions. To be successful, functional requirements must be tightly defined."
> —DAVID D'INNOCENZO, PRESIDENT & CEO, NETWORKINGSPS, LLC

In a special report issued recently, Binod Taterway, CEO of Blue Canopy, suggests a broader, more holistic approach to outsourcing transition and management. Just as Linda Cohen recommended the creation of an ongoing operations management team, Taterway recommends the creation of a service management office, or SMO. "Many organizations manage outsourcing relationships at the procurement level," a process that does not work well, Taterway says. "An SMO is an operating entity that works with vendors on a daily basis to ensure successful service delivery.

"Depending upon the size of the outsource deal and number of participants, the level of your SMO could be departmental, interdepartmental, or enterprisewide. It also needs to include representatives from your vendor or service providers," Taterway says.

Taterway also recommends creating a "rulebook," that is, an operating-level agreement (OLA) defining how both parties should operate. While SLAs define the structure of performance, monitoring, measuring, and reviewing, an OLA, or rulebook, defines the "how" of working together. "For example," Taterway states, "the rulebook provides a mechanism to recover from an incident. It describes an approach to triage and recovery. Over time, the rulebook becomes the true 'rules-in-use' by which the organization supports its service delivery."

Attorney Brad Peterson has created a comprehensive outline entitled "Outsourcing, Maximizing Value and Avoiding Pitfalls" (see Chapter 15 of this book for information on how to order a copy). In this wide-ranging outline, Peterson covers success factors, transition structure, definitions, and task lists for the contract phase, and he recommends that both the vendor and the organization consider 11 key points, a few of which are

- *Describing services.* The services can be described in many ways, each of which is more or less appropriate depending on how service levels are defined and how the services are priced. These ways include

  - Resource availability, e.g., full-time equivalent personnel available per month or machines or processing capacity to be available

  - Tasks, e.g., send payroll checks, process new-hire data, fulfill consumers' orders, or install new software releases

  - Projects, e.g., designing, developing, and testing new software applications

  - Additional services to be determined by the parties

  - Quality assurance procedures

  - Control processes and procedures

  - Dragnet provisions, e.g., "all functions being provided by the outsourced function during the 12-month period prior to the effective date, whether or not described in this agreement"

- *IT capabilities.* The vendor's information technology capabilities are critical to the success of any outsourcing transaction, not merely for IT outsourcing transactions. IT provides

  - The quality and repeatability of processes and methodologies

  - The data link between the customer and the vendor

  - Rapid and accurate information about the outsourced function

- *Exclusivity.* Some outsourcing arrangements give the vendor the exclusive right to provide the outsourced services to the organization. These arrangements are referred to as "exclusive" or "requirements" contracts. Other agreements allow the organization to use multiple vendors.

- *Changes.* A flexible framework to handle changes without high risk for either party is needed. The key provisions include

  - A process for managing changes in service requirements

  - The organization's right to change the services being provided

  - The organization's right to change the priorities of the project

  - Responsibility for changing services based on changes in laws

  - The obligation to provide services to newly acquired entities and divested entities

  - Responsibility for identifying and documenting changes and proposing contract modifications

- *Disaster recovery.* This includes provisions to prevent disruption in services as the result of a disaster or similar adverse event, including

  - *Planning requirement.* The vendor may be required to conform to a plan attached to the contract, or merely to have a plan in place.

  - *Testing requirement.* The vendor may be required to test its disaster recovery plan periodically.

  - *Standby or backup facilities.* The vendor may be required to provide or demonstrate standby or backup facilities for mission-critical functions.

- *Implementation*. The vendor may agree to certain constraints on its implementation of disaster recovery plans or to implement disaster recovery plans when requested by the customer organization.

- *Priority*. If a disaster occurs, the customer organization wants priority over, or at least equal status with, the vendor's other customers for some or all of its functions.

- *Costs*. The outsourcing contract should allocate the costs of implementing the disaster recovery plan.

Peterson also recommends developing a yardstick or measurement process by which the performance of the vendor is evaluated. "The key issues in choosing a measurement process," Peterson recommends, "include accuracy, cost, and visibility, that is, real-time access to data and the ability to audit historical data."

The legal input during the transition phase is complex and essential. In addition to the issues mentioned here, consideration must be given to taxes, "other" expenses (e.g., travel), invoicing, payment scheduling, layoffs (e.g., the WARN Act (The Worker Adjustment and Retraining Notification Act), the Equal Employment Opportunity Commission, the Americans with Disabilities Act), stay bonuses, outplacement, retraining, the effects that the outsourcing initiative may have on any collective bargaining agreements that are in place, and much more. If your organization does not have an outsourcing attorney, get one.

IT TAKES A TEAM

The transition period is tumultuous, and having the right plan with the right team members, ready to design and support the transformation, is critical. This phase is a complete and total paradigm shift for your organization, and it requires a strong strategy and an organizationwide communication and education program to create the organizational readiness and acceptance for this shift.

It is during this stage that your team must step up, join forces, and make the transformation happen. A strong strategy will be your foundation, but excellent change management skills and open communication, especially as it relates to expectations, timing, pricing, and the human element, are crucial to your success. Use these skills and the skills and tools that follow to smooth out your path, so that you can reap the rewards of your outsourcing program.

PART 3

COMMITMENT TO SUCCEED

Once you have learned enough about outsourcing to know that you want to begin the process for your organization, it is time to learn just how much you do not yet know. On that point, a recent study revealed that 70 percent of the respondents had had significant negative experiences with outsourcing projects. These organizations are now exercising greater caution in approaching their outsourcing initiatives; their "negative experiences" were largely related to the "surprise" factor: hidden costs in outsourcing, differences in expectations, and fundamental yet often overlooked differences between product outsourcing and outsourcing service functions.

To make your outsourcing initiative completely successful, you have to build the right team of the right people with the right skills, and you must help them learn how to lead this change within your organization. There are many new skills to learn, new hurdles to overcome, new cultural and style differences to identify, and specific success factors that will turn your organization's outsourcing initiative into a smoothly operating machine.

The following chapters will provide you with real-time advice on making your outsourcing project accomplish more than you thought possible.

CHAPTER 7

BUILDING
YOUR TEAM

With any organizational transition, there comes an opportunity to make needed changes, experience the optimism of projected growth, and benefit from the inspiration of working with a reenergized team to deliver results that will make a difference to your organization. Transitions are also periods of increased vulnerability, as everything is different: your role as manager or executive, your working relationships with your senior management, your team, and your goals. Building the right team during the transition to outsourcing a function or department requires focus, an eye on the future, and die-hard optimism. It starts with the basics.

TEAM BUILDING: THE BASICS

Before we can identify the right in-house team, we must have an understanding of a "team" in its most fundamental sense: A team is a group of people working together toward a common goal. At this point in your transition to outsourcing, the members of your leadership team and everyone reporting to them may be *on* a team, but not functioning *as* a team. The most successful organizations in any transition (merger, acquisition, or outsourcing) build a team of enabled individuals collaborating to reach common goals. The foundation of building a high-performance team to support your outsourcing initiative includes

• Clarification of the goals

• Identification of the issues that inhibit the team from reaching the goals (including technical skills, business experience, people skills, and so on)

• Addressing the issues and removing of the barriers to enable each participant to reach her or his goals

The difficulty in implementing these three steps is directly related to your employees' fear, uncertainty, and doubt (FUD), their aversion to change, and the stages of team development.

Several models of team development exist, many of which are similar in suggesting that the process of working together occurs in four predictable stages:

1. *Honeymoon stage.* The team is busy dealing with the issues of inclusion.

2. *Honeymoon-is-over stage.* The team is busy dealing with the issues of leadership, power, and control.

3. *Getting to work.* The team is addressing the issue of unity and harmony.

4. *Delivering results.* The team is finally working on the common goals with a sense of identity.

During the honeymoon stage, team members reassess one another through the filters of FUD and change. Members tend to compare one another's similarities and differences, often with strong judgments attached, leading to apprehension and conflict as these comparisons surface within the team. During this stage, each team member works through the issues of inclusion (am I accepted here?), the ROI of being on this team (what price do I have to pay to be on this team?), hierarchy (who is the leader?), and deciding if he or she really wants to be on this team at all (is the leader competent?). As team members consider these matters, they spend more time soliciting information from their managers for structure and guidance, and less time working; this stage has an extremely low team productivity level. The amount of time your team spends in this stage of near inertia can be significantly reduced through frequent communication, open dialogue, clear structures, and rebuilding of trust.

During the honeymoon-is-over stage, team members engage in conflict over power, leadership, decision making, and control. Members may be more outspoken in communicating their feelings to one another, as well as to their outsourcing partners; however, they still view themselves as part of the "old-world team" rather than part of the new team. Decisions do not come easily within the group as team members struggle for position in an effort to establish themselves based on both credibility and value in relation to other team members and the team leader. While clarity of purpose increases from the previous stage, many uncertainties persist. Working through the inevitable conflict, unavoidable at this stage, includes each team member's consideration of autonomy, control, support, and influence.

Teams are often stuck in this stage, evidenced by poor behavior and diminished productivity levels. While productivity in this stage is low, the energy of the team is high as its members try to answer their own questions about autonomy (how will I gain independence?), control (how much control do I have in this new team?), support (who supports me; whom do I support?), and influence (how much influence do I have on this new team?).

To help your team move through this process quickly, you should develop a process for joint problem solving based on an agreement to work creatively together. Become receptive to the opinions and recommendations of others (no matter how busy you are), commit to teamwork founded on mutual respect, and pledge to find the *what*-is-right answer (rather than the *who*-is-right answer). This will help to establish a pathway for team standards based on differing viewpoints, help the decision-making process become increasingly objective, and support collaboration as a team custom.

When you reach the getting to work stage, you will see an increase in productivity and an increase in relationships built on trust. The team finally becomes cohesive; team members discover that they have much in common with one another, and they become more comfortable in appreciating, rather than judging, their differences. Agreement and consensus are largely formed throughout the team, and roles and responsibilities are clear and accepted. Team members are committed to working together, while still rebuilding trust. To move through this stage effectively, continue the open discussions regarding the team members' concerns, encourage members to participate wholeheartedly, frequently give positive and useful feedback, support collaborative decision making, and delegate as much as possible.

Upon finally reaching the delivering results stage, team members have learned how to work together as a fully functioning, high-powered team. The team is more strategically aware; it knows not only what to do, but how and why. Its members now have a shared vision and a common mission, and they are able to operate well on their own. They have a sense of identity as a team and a commitment to one another to reach the goals. The team is highly productive and effective; at this point, differences and conflict are seen as a way to generate creativity in the problem-solving process rather than simply a complaint platform. It is at this point that your team is actually delivering results.

Additionally, the success characteristics of a high-powered team include having and understanding a clear mission; demonstrating mutual support and respect; and having clear roles and responsibilities, open and honest communications, individual competence, and optimism. Of all the characteristics listed here, optimism is the most important: Your team must expect to win.

Optimism is about an individual's inclination to anticipate the best possible outcome for actions or events. The main difference between optimists and pessimists is how they explain setbacks to themselves: An optimist will assume that "I can do something to change this negative situation," whereas a pessimist will be likely to assume that "nothing I do will make any difference at all, so why bother?" Optimists believe that negative circumstances are temporary, and pessimists see negative circumstances as permanent.

When helping your team through the sequential and predictable stages of development, integrate the learning of the success characteristics, especially optimism, into the mix. Optimistic employees accept change more readily and move through the stages more quickly.

THE TEAM

Understanding the basic team-building concepts is critical to prepare the operations management team (OMT), the senior leadership team, and the remaining teams for the evaluation of their suitability in the new world order. Far from clearing the slate and starting from scratch, you must be judicious in the selection of your OMT, as well as the structure of your entire organization, and you must create a process by which you synchronize your team with your goals. The strategy for building your team can be completed in three stages: the *What*, the *Where*, and the *How:*

- The *What* process is the identification of the current organizational situation—what exists now, operationally and culturally, technically and behaviorally.

- The *Where* process is the identification of where you'd like to be in terms of organizational size, shape, culture—and results.

- The *How* process is the strategy for moving from the What to the Where quickly and effectively.

THE WHAT

We have all observed executives, when entering a new situation, jumping in and cleaning house. For example, the new CFO of a high-tech organization in the San Francisco Bay Area, immediately after signing his employment contract but prior to meeting his future senior staff, had them all dismissed. This incoming CFO had no idea, really, if he was discharging the very talent that he would need in order to succeed—but he wanted his "own" team, regardless. His ability to deliver value to his new organization was slowed to a crawl as an entire new senior staff became integrated into the organization, its culture, its opportunities, its vulnerabilities, and the stages of team development.

Conversely, there are managers who maintain a team in place for far longer than is practical. The result of postponing the evaluation and management of individual and team performance also is a delay in value delivery, as the manager's time is continually spent monitoring the work of employees whose jobs may have simply outgrown them. Somewhere between cleaning house and maintaining the status quo is a process for learning about your employees in the current setting. The What of your organization begins with an assessment of each individual in more global terms, that is, a general evaluation of both technical and behavioral performance:

- *Skill and knowledge.* What skills and knowledge, background and education, has each individually used successfully so far in her or his career with your organization?

- *Style.* How does each individual respond to problems and challenges as they arise? How does the individual respond to changes in operations, taking risks, or complying with new procedures and structures? There are assessments to measure this; see Chapter 15 for recommendations. The purpose of these assessments is simply to determine *how* each individual responds to these factors, and the results should be used to help each individual shift to more effective response styles. These assessments, however, should not be used as a tool to rule anyone *out*; they are only an evaluation of style, not a judgment of style.

- *Focus.* Does each individual understand his or her goals, prioritize tasks in support of those goals, and stay the course?

- *Collaboration.* How are the rapport-building skills of each individual? Does each individual demonstrate the ability to lead when required and to follow when necessary? What type of decision-making style does each individual demonstrate, and how easy (or difficult) is it to work with each person?

- *Trust.* Trust is a delicate issue, and in this case, we are speaking more about the individual's past performance as a forecast of the predictability of her or his future behavior: Can you comfortably predict that each individual will deliver results? Is each individual committed to the success of the organization? Is each individual willing to keep the commitments that she or he makes?

Another important part of the What analysis is the employee's perception of the circumstances. To gather input and show each team member support, each individual should be asked the following questions:

- What do you believe to be the strengths of this new organizational structure?

- What concerns do you have about this new organizational structure?

- What would you change or improve?

- What can we offer you that will help you be more successful?

In my recent book, *How to Shine at Work* (McGraw-Hill), there are a number of tools—far too many to reprint here—that will help organizations and individuals evaluate the What, shift their behavioral styles, and learn new technical skills. Once the What piece has been identified, you should move on to the Where.

THE WHERE

In the most straightforward sense, the Where is a description of where you want your organization to be, the point at which you can say, "This outsourcing initiative is successful." Before you can make that statement, you must refine your definition of success for your organization.

In addition to the success definition documented during the vendor-selection process, creating a comprehensive vision statement for your organization will clarify your Where. Your vision, a statement of what you see as possible for your organization, will be supported by the organization's mission statement (see the How, discussed next). This visionary process allows you to ask yourself and your organization, "What is our preferred future?" In addition to being the primary communication of organizational goals, your vision statement is a critical part of your strategy, and should include

- What you want to see in the future: your definition of success

- The new culture and environment of the organization: standards you will maintain

- References to the high priorities of customers, employees, vendors, shareholders, and parent companies

- Specific forward-thinking, optimistic communication to your organization of what is possible, in turn creating an environment of motivation so that people are drawn toward participation

• A precise and practical guide for the actions of all involved

The benefits of using this process to define your Where include providing a big-picture perspective to all employees, allowing the organization to align the people, ideas, and attitudes with the inspired vision of success. If your employees can quote your new vision statement and your leadership team walks the talk of your new vision statement, then you have done well; if your vision statement is nothing more than a wall plaque, your organization lacks the cohesive vision to become effective and successful in the outsourcing endeavor, and your team will lack the ability to work toward common goals.

THE HOW

The How of building your team is the strategy to fill the gap between where you are right now and where you want to be in order to experience and sustain success. The employee skill base (from the What evaluation) and the vision statement (from the Where evaluation), along with the success factors identified during your vendor-selection process, will be the basis of your How strategy identification as it relates to your team.

A good team is driven by a mission—that is, what the team intends to do to make the organizational vision materialize. With the vision (the Where) in mind, each team and function creates its own mission statement that fits into the organizational vision; ultimately, each individual will create a mission statement that serves as part of his or her performance index—what that individual will do to transform the organization's vision into reality.

As a supporting document for the team mission statements clarifying what will be done to reach the vision of success, each team and each individual must create a valid index of what it will take to be successful in the mission to reach success. This index is a simple outline of what it takes to be a high performer in a specific job or function, covering the business and behavioral aspects of each job. It differs from a conventional job description in that it is much shorter and emphasizes results rather than activities. The factors in a good performance index include

- *Desired outcomes.* Identification of the most important mission-critical business results associated with the specific job

- *Actions.* Identification of the actions that are necessary to drive those achievements

- *Behavioral skills.* Identification of those interpersonal and internal management abilities that are necessary to achieve the desired outcomes, including such things as self-awareness, self-motivation, influence, conflict management, and team building (including the elements of emotional intelligence, identified in the book by that name written by Daniel Goleman)

- *Technical abilities.* Identification of the technical skills necessary to deliver key results, e.g., computer capabilities

- *Experience and/or education.* Identification of those areas of expertise required to deliver results

This index of what is required for success allows each job function to be monitored against a plan in an easy and collaborative way. Given this information, you are ready to evaluate the best team members for your organization as you push forward, while also identifying those individuals who may need additional training and those whose performance may no longer work in the new world order. Building a great team takes courage and action. If you follow the process outlined here, each action you take in building your team will be aligned with your business strategy, will allow you to get all executives and employees on the same page, and will move you toward the success you seek.

CHAPTER 8

NEW SKILLS NEEDED

In his book The *First 90 Days* (HBS Press, 2003), author Michael Watkins identified a breakeven point at which "leaders have contributed as much to their new organizations as they have consumed," that is, the point in time when the value consumed in the form of salary, benefits, learning time, informational meetings, and so on is equal to the value created (the results delivered). The Watkins study of 210 executives estimated that newly hired or promoted managers work for 6.2 months, or approximately 186 days, before reaching that breakeven point. The key, then, for the leader of a new outsourcing team, in-house, onsite, or off-site, as well as for the entire organization, is to manage the value-consuming stage and accelerate the value-delivery stage for everyone involved.

We recognize that in an outsourcing initiative, there are many opportunities for failure that are related to structure, agreements, strategy, and contracts. In addition, there are potential failure opportunities in the subtle interaction between the organizational situation (opportunities, new expectations, new reporting structure, and so on) and the individual team members' strengths, skills, values, vulnerabilities, and loyalty (see Chapter 7). The skills and competencies needed now for the executive leadership, the operations management team (OMT), and staff members have shifted. At the top of the organization, the executive team must incorporate a different style of leading, and the management staff must incorporate a different style of managing process and people, while transforming the organizational culture, developing a new political structure, and reaching new goals.

When asked about the underlying reasons for outsourcing failure, Phillip Hatch of Ventoro.com stated, "The ultimate success or failure of an outsourcing strategy hinges on the performance of the implementing executive. Engagements that do not succeed are tripped up 52 percent of the time by problems exclusive to the organization." The essential elements of focus for executives during any transition are based on solid leadership.

NEW SKILLS FOR LEADERSHIP

When it comes to leadership, no single approach fits all situations, and during a transition, it is particularly important to understand which approach best fits which situation. In Daniel Goleman's white paper "Leadership That Gets Results," (*Harvard Business Review*), six primary leadership styles were identified. These styles, Coercive, Pacesetting, Affiliative, Democratic, Coaching, and Authoritative, were identified through a research study conducted by Hay/McBer that involved 3,871 executives. The results of the survey suggested that great leaders actually adapt their style to each situation. Goleman's conclusions from the executive style survey are summarized as follows:

- *Coercive.* This style demands immediate compliance—the "do what I tell you" approach. The good news is that this style works well in a crisis, and the bad news is "the negative long-term impact of insensitivity to morale and employees' feelings." This is the least effective of Goleman's six identified styles, for any situation.

- *Pacesetting.* This style sets high standards for performance—the "do as I do, *now*" approach. The good news is that you will get quick results from a highly competent staff; the bad news is that this style works well only with a highly competent staff. This style is not recommended, especially during a transition.

- *Affiliative.* This style creates harmony and builds emotional bonds—the "people come first" approach. The good news is that the focus is on employees' emotional concerns. This positive approach helps to create a strong sense of loyalty, motivates people during stressful circumstances, and leads to the repair of broken trust. The bad news is that this style can allow "performance problems to go uncorrected in favor of the emotional wellbeing of the employees." This style may be a positive leadership style during a transition, especially when balanced with results delivery.

- *Democratic.* This style prefers consensus through participation—the "what do you think?" approach. The good news is that in a transitional situation, using a democratic approach can be positive—you build trust and employee commitment through the solicitation of ideas and buy-in. The bad news is that consensus is "time-consuming and a possible drag on real-time decision making."

- *Coaching.* This style develops people for the future—the "try this" approach. The good news is this style works well to help employees improve their performance or develop long-term strengths. The bad news is that this approach "works well [only] with people who want to be coached."

- *Authoritative.* This style mobilizes people toward a vision—the "come with me" approach. The good news is that when change requires a new vision or when clear direction is needed, this style gets the job done. While this style does not work well with an "authoritative leader and a peer-group of equally experienced, talented, and knowledgeable people," it is the most strongly positive leadership style, especially for a company that is in transition.

Whatever your leadership style, new skills that need to be incorporated during this transition and beyond include providing specific direction, developing an environment of motivation, demonstrating optimism, leading by example, making the right moves, and measuring your progress against predetermined standards or metrics, all of which will allow you to deliver results beyond expectations. Specifically,

- *Providing specific direction.* Leaders provide direction for their entire organization by developing and supporting a vision and mission for themselves and their organization (see Chapter 7 for more on this). During this time of change from old to new, the leadership must provide specific direction, yet not micromanage. The new skill to learn is how to provide unambiguous direction while continually seeking input, innovation, and a better way. Leaders must be much more adept at communicating clearly, inspiring trust and respect, and adapting their leadership style to fit the situation, while guiding the organization to deliver results on time, on budget, and on standard.

- *Leading by example.* Especially in the face of change, leaders must stand for values that do not change. Great leadership requires high standards, valuing a rich and diverse workforce, and genuine humility (not being puffed up). There can be no "do as I say, not as I do" here; you must keep the commitments you make and share decision making with others throughout the organization. Successful leaders understand the difference between strength and power, with strength referring to your capacity for effective action and power referring to your ability to control (see Goleman's reference to the Coercive leadership style). It is the leadership of the organization that sets the standards of behavior and performance (culture), sets the expectations for success, and then holds people accountable for their actions.

- *Motivation.* Leaders create an environment of motivation that helps people work their best, even in the face of change. In the new ever-changing outsourcing transition, learning how to sustain your own motivation will make it easier for you to create the healthy motivational environment for your staff. Lead with respect and encouragement, especially for those who are willing to adapt quickly to change, in an effort to reduce the fear-based political structure and transform the environment to one of empowered and inspired teams.

- *Optimism.* Optimism is simply a tendency to anticipate the best possible outcome for everything—the tendency to believe, expect, or hope that things will turn out well. A realistic, yet positive outlook for the future is necessary for leading your organization and reaching your new goals. Martin Seligman, in his book *Learned Optimism* (Free Press, 1998), studied the level of optimism shown by U.S. presidential candidates between 1900 and 1984. American voters chose the more optimistic-sounding candidate in 18 out of 22 elections. Why? Because voters, not unlike executives, managers, and staff, prefer to follow a leader who has a vision of opportunity and hope, and respond well to leaders who send these messages. Great leaders demonstrate a positive and confident outlook on the world, and that approach will trickle down throughout the organization.

"Optimism is essential to achievement and it is also the foundation of courage and true progress."
—Nicholas Murray Butler

- *Making the right moves.* Making all the right moves becomes an option only within the scope of a strong strategy. The strategy is based on your vision and mission (see Chapter 7 and the section "Strategic Management" later in this chapter), and then the tasks and actions that you will undertake to fulfill your mission.

- *Measuring your progress.* Measure, monitor, and report (MMR). Your organization and your vendor must understand not only what needs to be done, but also by when, by whom, and how well. Then metrics with which to measure productivity, quality, service, and behavioral skills required can become part of your overall success strategy and can be included in your performance index (see Chapter 7).

  In Chapters 5 and 7, you identified what must be accomplished to ensure success for your organization; now you must determine how your teams, internal and external, will be measured in this new dynamic. The vendor metrics are in place for the product or service delivery; collaborate with your in-house team, using your performance index and a predetermined MMR process to ensure that you are actually measuring the right things, using the right benchmarks, at the right time—and that the right people know what is working and what is not.

In addition to measuring productivity, quality, and service (the technical end of the spectrum), put metrics in place to measure the softer side of the continuum as outlined in Chapter 7. Consider such things as streamlining, standardization, knowing the right processes, risk taking, creativity, building trust, and working well together.

Dick LeFave at Nextel frequently has his group measure against the plan, in a process called "true-ups." "We true up every month. The first year, you always struggle over service. When they don't hit the mark, it's an escalation factor. They want good press, but they have to deliver. We also hold quarterly senior management meetings, we listen to the stories—there are billions of dollars, lots of delivery, and when these deals go bad, they can take a lot with them."

The goal of every optimistic leader is to achieve results beyond expectations. This organizational transformation to an outsourced model is an opportunity to make that happen, and learning and applying an updated set of leadership skills will guarantee your results.

NEW SKILLS FOR MANAGERS

Outsourcing is often discussed only in terms of organizational cost savings, yet how outsourcing affects employees who remain in-house is equally important. Managers staying on in the new world order find that their workloads do not necessarily decrease; in fact, the result is usually quite the opposite. Suddenly managers are faced with the challenges of managing remote teams of people, taking on new responsibilities, managing change, and shifting the focus from knowledge capital or process knowledge to outcome management. This may necessitate that managers acquire, in addition to their subject-matter expertise, additional expertise in areas such as risk management, change management, decision management, and strategic management.

Often organizations have an expectation that their existing management staff, which was previously responsible for managing the operations of a product or service delivery function, will automatically become expert at leaving the operations management to the outsourcer, and will shift effortlessly to managing the expected outcome. However, managers who were previously responsible for operational performance ("if we follow procedures, we'll get the results") may not be the right people to fit the new profile of an outsourcing manager.

Linda Cohen of Gartner, Inc. states,

> You can't mess with managing the *how*, you must manage the *what*, or the outcome. If you leave the external operations management with the people who used to manage it internally, you may end up with an even larger problem. For example, if you outsource payroll, the best manager of the outsource project is probably not the displaced outsource manager—he will most likely be measuring the *how* of the payroll process rather than the *what*.

Once they are operating in an outsourcing environment, managers find that there is a different set of expectations, requiring new and different skills. However, when good managers fail in an outsourcing situation, there is often a troubling misalignment between the typical outsourcing strategy and the current level of management skill. This misalignment occurs when the in-house managers are unprepared, untrained, and overworked in their new roles. The skills and processes required to manage a vendor relationship are rarely inherent in the organization, yet most managers will be reluctant to say, "I need to learn these new skills."

It is important for organizations to create a career path to develop and maintain the skills required to manage a portfolio of external vendors for the benefit of the business.

RISK MANAGEMENT

Risk management is a practice that offers processes, methods, and tools for managing risks in a project or organization. It provides a closely controlled environment for proactive decision making and continuously assesses what could go wrong, in order to determine which risks are highest priority and implementing strategies to deal with those risks.

As seen in Chapter 3, the risks of any outsourcing initiative can be overwhelming. In larger organizations with poor communication systems, outsourcing decisions often occur independently of one another, resulting in potential risks that are not fully communicated or understood. For example, a hospital in the United Kingdom was reportedly having all the windows replaced in an older wing of the building, while at the same time another team was making plans to demolish that same wing and build a newer structure. No communication equals big risks.

Managers in the new outsourced environment must have a comprehensive understanding of the overall outsourcing initiative, including the potential risks of outsourcing, while also having a framework for ongoing risk management over the complete life cycle of the contract.

CHANGE MANAGEMENT

Change management is the process, tools, and techniques engaged to manage the people side of transforming processes in order to achieve the desired outcome. To be effective, the management of change must include the individual, the team, and the organization. There are many models of change for organizations, yet there is one fundamental theme: It is about learning to do something different in the course of reaching your goals. Change is the result of an organizational learning process that centers on these questions:

- In order to grow as an organization and as individuals within the organization, what do we need to maintain and what do we need to change?

- How can we manage this change while maintaining the harmony and values that we hold as individuals and as an organization?

For individuals and teams to answer these questions, it must be understood that change takes place through *learning* on three levels: the individual, the team, and the organization. The process of change management will address learning needs on all three levels.

CHANGE MANAGEMENT AND THE INDIVIDUAL

During this time of transition and uncertainty, individual success is primarily determined by the ability to adapt to change. For each individual, the ability to identify and manage his or her resistance to change is directly related to what that individual has to gain or lose because of the change. An effective manager in a time of change knows how to help assess the individual resistance of his or her team members and knows how to help the team members identify obstacles, plan for action, build commitment, and rapidly make adjustments to keep the momentum going. This skill may not have been required of a successful manager in the old-world process-driven management practice, yet it is a key to success in the new environment.

CHANGE MANAGEMENT AND THE TEAM

As each team works through the stages of development (see Chapter 7), the manager must clarify the expectations, ensure that the team understands those expectations at the level of detail that the project requires, and prepare the team to reach the goals. Managing change on a team includes other strategic drivers, personalities, and politics, all of which can affect the ability of the team to thrive. For some individuals, change is natural and acceptable; for others, change is risky, frightening, and intolerable.

Change in the team sense is a learning event: The team *learns* how to change based on guidance from a manager who is knowledgeable in adult learning processes. (See Fig. 8.1) The efficient and productive manager must understand the basic principles of adult learning (formally termed *andragogy*) and incorporate these principles into the management process to help your team move more

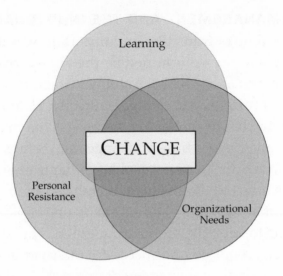

Figure 8.1   Components of change.

quickly into a results-delivery stage. The basic principles of adult learning include an understanding that

- Adults are *autonomous* and need to be free to direct themselves. As an effective manager in the new environment, you must actively involve team members in the learning process, serving as a facilitator as well as a manager. In addition to soliciting input, the manager must demonstrate to the team how the change they are facing relates to reaching their goals.

- Adults have accumulated a foundation of *life experiences and knowledge* that may include work-related activities, family responsibilities, and previous education. Because a typical adult needs to connect her or his new learning (in this case, learning to change) to this extensive knowledge/experience base, managers have to draw out adults' experience and knowledge that might be relevant to the new tasks or desired outcomes. Adults find the value of *experience* in learning to be motivational.

- Adults are *goal-oriented*. Once the team understands the goal, its members can work together to define, organize, and structure the elements required for success.

- Adults are *relevancy-oriented*. They must see a reason for learning something; in this case, they must see a reason for learning how to change. Learning must be germane to their work or other responsibilities to be of value to them. A good manager must identify objectives for the team that include concepts that are directly related to their success.

- Adults are *practical* and will focus directly on the aspects of their responsibilities that are most useful to them in their own work.

- Adults need to be shown *respect*. Managers must acknowledge the wealth of experience that team members bring to the new environment. Team members must be shown respect for their contributions and must be allowed to voice their constructive opinions.

- Adults require an *environment of motivation*. In addition to the previous points, adults are motivated when they are able to develop new relationships at work, reach their own goals, have opportunities for personal development, and experience intellectual stimulation. The good manager in the new environment knows how to develop an environment in which employees *want* to learn how to change.

CHANGE MANAGEMENT AND THE ORGANIZATION

Just as there are different leadership styles for different circumstances, different transition situations require different change recipes. Even with the differences in the approach to change management and the organization, however, all change paths converge at one basic point: unfreezing the organization. In order to make change happen, teams and their managers must get unstuck. To do this, managers must clearly understand what resistance looks like, and must formulate a strategy to address it quickly and efficiently. Failure to do so will keep the organization frozen, and progress is not likely to occur.

Mike Matteo is vice president of operations for 360Sourcing.com, a product-sourcing company focused on consumer and commercial hard goods. With over 20 years of experience with supply-chain, logistics, and operations leadership, he has seen his share of change-related organizational issues. "Don't squander the opportunity to grow," Matteo says.

> When we're working together, we advocate full and open disclosure of everything. We show you everything related to costs and fees. So, when I show you that you can save 30 percent with a manufacturing structure in China, and I give you the backup to prove it, and you are afraid to change, you are squandering the opportunity to improve.

Organizations with a high level of resistance have very few "change agents" on staff and may require a more radical approach to breaking the dominant (resistant) culture. To convert the organizational culture to one centered on change, start with the resistance nearest the top and determine what type of reorganization may be required. The entire senior team must be ready for change, ready to lead the charge, and ready to learn the new skills required for success. This adjustment is not a temporary quick fix; it is a permanent culture change (including political shifts). Have your organizational leaders become the change that they want to see in others.

DECISION MANAGEMENT

In most organizations, the existing decision model is based on process, whereas the decision model of an outsourced organization must be based on outcomes. To be a good manager in the new order is to know what is important, what is probable, and how to take advantage of business control strategies so that you can consistently produce the best results.

STRATEGIC MANAGEMENT

Strategic *thinking* as a part of the decision management process is the assessment of priorities through the filter of three key requirements: a definite purpose or desired outcome, an understanding of the environment and culture (especially of resistance factors that may impede your progress to the desired outcome), and creativity in developing effective responses to those factors.

Strategic *management* is the application of strategic *thinking* to the vision and mission of leading an organization, especially an organization in transition. Strategic management includes the identification of constantly changing external factors (e.g., customer requirements, competition, regulation, new technology, remote teams, and so on), the creation of a competitive strategy to achieve the goals, and the development of an organizational structure that will be ready to deploy resources to successfully carry out the organization's competitive strategy.

Strategic management was not a requirement in the old world order, where the battle cry was, "This is the way we've always handled it." An outsourcing initiative brings your company to a new world order, one that requires strategic management: an adaptive approach to creating a game plan for running the business, satisfying customers, and achieving targets.

RETHINKING THE ROLE OF MANAGEMENT IN AN OUTSOURCING TRANSITION

In order to reach the breakeven point of the value consumed–value delivered challenge, leaders and managers in the new organizational culture must learn to enthusiastically formulate, evaluate, and implement strategies for both new and existing businesses. This is possible only when the organization is able to change and adapt quickly, and it is possible only in an organization that understands change through the filter of learning. Successful leaders and managers will help create a set of values and beliefs that resonate with employees, and will focus on the following points:

- Respect and support for their employees as they work their way through the change, while concentrating on performance requirements and results delivery.

- Leading by example: becoming a catalyst for change when change is needed. –As Mahatma Gandhi said, "We must become the change we want to see."

- Creating a climate of trust in the organization through frequent communication.

- Demonstrating the value of the diversity of your employees' background, education, contributions, and ability to adapt to change.

- Encouraging creativity among teams; creating an environment of motivation, training, and freedom to achieve goals,

- Keeping their eyes on the outcomes.

The new skills needed for success will be different for each manager, executive, and organization. During any phase of the outsourcing process, successful managers will be those who are willing to take prudent risks, are able to quickly modify their strategies and operating practices in support of the mission, and are adept at instilling trust and confidence in all employees.

CHAPTER 9

CRITICAL SUCCESS FACTORS FOR MANAGERS

In most discussions about the successful management of an outsourcing initiative, the principal focus of attention is the performance of the vendor. While vendor performance is certainly critical to the success of an outsourcing program, perhaps of even greater importance is the management of the outsourcing relationships once the contract is signed. Success factors for managers of outsourcing initiatives include the shift from managing activities to managing outcomes and building cooperation and collaboration across the miles (or across the street) based on well-defined management principles, with clear accountabilities and unambiguous processes to support the delivery of profitable results. As teams are scattered across the country or the world, key success factors for managers include those discussed here.

RESULTS MANAGEMENT

The normal challenges of leading a traditional team on-site are easy compared to the challenges of managing a remote team. These include the complexity of being geographically separated; managers need to work across time zones, across functions, and with diverse cultural foundations, while respecting the vendor's business process and managing the outcome. Linda Cohen of Gartner, Inc. adds, "Don't tell the outsourcer how to do their business," recommending instead that managers learn how to "balance trust and control."

A widespread concern that is shared by managers and executives is the process-oriented question, "How do I know that my vendor is really working when I'm not there to watch it?" The answer is, "You won't know until you start measuring results." Since it is easy to confuse *activity* or process management with *accomplishments*, a key factor in management success is to shift that focus.

Through the contract process, the organization has presented the vendor with specific, measurable, and attainable goals: Your vendor knows what must be done, by when, and how well. It is important that the organization and vendor agree on a shared definition of the deliverables and timetable to ensure that everyone is moving toward the same targets and using the same metrics to measure the results.

A manager's value to an organization with an outsourcing initiative may be more as a coach and mentor and less as an overseer. This shift from "surveillance management" to a performance-based approach contributes to the vendor's improved productivity. This measurement of outcomes must be conducted at frequent and regular intervals to keep the relationship on track.

BUILDING TRUST

Successfully working with teams, in-house or outsourced, depends largely on collaboration. Collaboration requires the sharing of information, knowledge, observations, and opinions with other team members. If we do not trust one another, then we will not collaborate with one another freely. Trust and collaboration are inseparable.

Communication builds trust; through communicating with people, we evaluate them to get a better sense of who they are and how they process information, and we attempt to understand their priorities. People who have opportunities to meet face to face have the luxury of the visual (i.e., observing body language in addition to the pace of speech, tone of voice, and words), allowing people to understand one another more quickly. In remote teams and off-site vendor relationships, team members have not had sufficient "face time," so the manager must facilitate this evaluation and analysis of style through forms of communication other than in person.

In short, good outsourcing managers understand that high-powered teamwork is contingent on collaboration, which relies on trust, which is developed through communication. Building trust also includes leading by example, keeping the commitments you make, demonstrating integrity, supporting the team, in-house and off-site, while keeping an eye on the desired outcome and monitoring against the metrics set during the contract phase.

CREATING A UNITED FRONT

In the turmoil of transition, it is very easy for vendor relationships to remain on the fringes of your organization. With strong support from the senior leadership team, a good outsourcing manager will strive to connect, or embed, the vendor into the organization. Work to eliminate the us-them syndrome, ensure that your vendor has access to appropriate resources, and create an incentive process (recognition, acknowledgment, and so on) that includes both vendors and internal team members. Remember that a good team can have a wide-ranging effect on vendors and others who come from outside the business.

COMMUNICATION:
THE HIGHWAY TO "NO SURPRISES"

Communication is one of the most important elements in guaranteeing a successful outsourcing program. For dealing with the issues of distance, a variety of tools are available today to make it easier than ever to collaborate, build trust, and communicate. An important issue for a manager is developing the balance between being informed (in touch, connected, and so on) and being a micromanaging annoyance.

In outsourcing situations, especially those at quite a physical distance, managers and on-site coworkers are often concerned with being able to get in touch with off-site workers in a timely manner. To lessen the concern about the timeliness of communications, managers can set standards for turnaround times, can set regular meetings, can shift the start-time schedules for on-site employees, and can share with off-site and in-house team members the best methods for taking advantage of distance and time zones. There are a number of online methods for keeping the communication lines open, including the following:

- *Threaded discussions.* Many software tools facilitate newsgroup-like discussions that allow team members to communicate on any topic at different times. Threaded discussion tools created on an intranet focus on specific issues and save the actual dialogue or exchange of ideas for later use.

- *Instant messaging.* Instant messaging (IM) can be a valuable tool for informal and quick conversations in the corporate world. Like threaded discussions, many IM tools can save the actual chat for later review. The downside of this method involves privacy issues, so before launching a companywide IM program, make sure that your confidential information is secure.

- *Web conferencing.* When real-time communication is needed, conference calls can be significantly enhanced with Web conferencing. Depending on the software, Web conferencing products may include collaboration features such as whiteboarding, file sharing, instant messaging, and cooperative editing.

- *Blogging.* Created through a process of instant publishing to a Web page, blogs typically contain short messages that appear in chronological order. Blogging was created as a way for people to record their daily work, personal experiences, or random thoughts, yet it is a good avenue for keeping teams and shifts of teams aware and informed.

- *Voice over IP.* Depending on bandwidth availability, teams may also want to consider voiceover IP. Voiceover IP, or VoIP, converts the voice signal from your telephone into a digital signal that travels over the Internet. That signal is converted back to voice at the receiving end, allowing you to speak to anyone with a regular phone number.

KNOWLEDGE INTEGRATION

A fundamental challenge in an outsourcing initiative is developing methods to build and maintain knowledge-based systems. Knowledge integration, or KI, is the job of recognizing how new and prior knowledge interact when you incorporate new information into a knowledge base to move you forward toward your goals.

A good outsourcing manager understands the value of both old and new, and works to integrate both on an incremental basis as bits and slices of knowledge are added to a growing body of knowledge. By identifying subtle conflicts and gaps in knowledge between vendor and organization, a manager who is well versed in KI facilitates the building of an in-house knowledge base on which you can grow.

VISITING YOUR VENDOR

Whether your vendor's team is on-site, off-site, or offshore, you should plan to visit its headquarters or operations facility regularly. Depending on the nature of your project, a substantial portion of the team may be based off-site; visiting that location allows the off-site team to know who you are, while allowing you to communicate your business expectations in person. According to Art Salyer of Trojan Batteries, "You must make a commitment to go there, wherever there is, even if it means a heavy travel schedule. You must have a personal connection with your vendor, and it can't be done entirely from a distance." Arrange for the appropriate people from your in-house team to make these trips with you, and budget for these visits as part of your overall project financial plan.

While most vendors appreciate having you visit their facilities, and while digital collaboration and information sharing are helpful, nothing can replace the interaction and relationship-building opportunities of occasional face-to-face meetings at organizational headquarters.

Invite your vendors in to meet the on-site team, see the location, and understand the culture of the organization more fully.

DEALING WITH CONFLICT

In any work environment, there will be disagreements, differences of opinion, diverse styles, delays, and errors, all contributing to the possible disruption of the work process in-house and off-site. Perhaps because on-site managers have previously been rewarded on the basis of process analytics, or perhaps because on-site managers mistakenly believe that their new vendors should be flawless, managers can fall into the trap of being unable to move past a problem. Moving toward a solution is critical to making an outsourcing relationship successful. Problems are inevitable—how you deal with the problems can make the difference between a comfortable and profitable relationship and a miserable association.

Successful managers will be aware that mistakes and misunderstandings will happen, and they will create a process by which these things can be resolved quickly:

1. *Proactive approaches to conflict pressure points.* Especially during the first year of an outsourcing contract, there will be points of conflict involving expectations, quality, outcomes, and so on. These flashpoints must be monitored and communicated upward through the organization, and must be reported back to the vendor on a regular basis in an effort to make the necessary shifts to accomplish the goals. The focus here is on the solution, so that the working relationship stays healthy and respectful.

2. *Handling personality clashes.* Sometimes because of cultural issues (see Chapter 11 for more on this) and sometimes because of work-style differences, employees may clash with their outsourced partners. The goal of conflict resolution between individuals is to find the best way to get to "*what* is right" rather than "*who* is right."

FEEDBACK AND SUPPORT

An important and often overlooked tool when working in an outsourcing situation is providing ongoing feedback and support. While we are quick to call attention to errors and inadequacies, many employees, both on-site and off-site, believe that they do not get enough feedback from managers on how well they are performing relative to their goals.

The process of giving and receiving feedback is one of the most important ways for learning new, more effective skills and behaviors. Remembering a few simple guidelines for giving feedback will make it easier:

- *Have regular meetings.* Regular meetings should be scheduled between managers and employees and between managers and outsourcing vendors to assess needs, give feedback, and discuss problems. This is an excellent opportunity to discuss the initially agreed-upon scope of work to be done, timelines, and deadlines.

- *Be specific.* Give specific, clear examples of the behavior or performance that is not working. It is all too easy to deny, defend, deflect, or simply ignore feedback when it is ambiguous.

- *Be descriptive, not judgmental.* Describe the behavior or performance in observable terms rather than using words that are evaluative. Judgmental or evaluative feedback crosses the line into the emotional arena, based on opinions, and opens the door to defensiveness and denial.

- *Consider timing.* Corrective feedback is most effective when it is given right after the performance or behavior occurs—privately (when there is time for discussion) and with respect.

Good feedback reduces the FUD factor in people—they will know where they stand. Feedback solves current problems and prepares us to resolve future problems; it builds trust, can strengthen relationships, and ultimately can improve work quality.

MASTERING THE FOUR KEYS TO SUCCESS

Success as an outsourcing manager may parallel success as an old-world manager in that ultimately you are measured by your results. How you reach those results as an outsourcing manager involves key shifts in management style; some of those shifts are external, and some are internal (personal). External shifts, as described earlier, are a change in your approach to people and outcome management.

Internal or personal shifts for a successful outsourcing manager include mastering the following qualities.

ACCOUNTABILITY

In the enlightening book The Oz Factor, authors Connor, Smith, and Hickman characterize the fine line between success and failure in any management capacity as being based on accountability. If you were to envision a horizontal success-failure line across a piece of paper, "below-the-line" behaviors would include

- Ignoring or denying a problem

- Refusing to step up because it's just "not my job"

- Finger pointing and blaming

- Waiting to be told what to do

- Playing "cover your tail"

- Waiting to see what will happen next

"Above-the-line" behaviors include *choosing* to see what is going on, taking ownership of the situation, creating a solution for the problem, and implementing that solution. When you accept full accountability for your thoughts, feelings, actions, and results, you will base your management style on integrity, and your teams will follow your lead. Anything less falls below the line and is a fast track to failure.

TRUST, AGAIN

While a good deal of effort will be expended in helping team members and vendors learn how to trust one another, the outsourcing manager must be able to earn and demonstrate trust as well.

Given all the effort that an outsourcing manager must apply in order to drive outcomes, attempting to control others may seem like a shortcut to the goal line. The problem is that attempting to control others demonstrates to them that you do not trust or respect them, and it squanders any opportunity for your employees to trust and respect you, ultimately slowing productivity.

If you maintain your integrity, keep the commitments you make, admit to your own mistakes, are fully accountable for yourself and your actions, and are willing to teach these same traits to your team, you will be building a foundation of trust and respect that will pull you forward.

ADAPTABILITY

The ability to adjust easily to changes and new conditions is imperative in the outsourcing manager's world. To be adaptable as a manager is to be open to new ideas and approaches, to be creative when problem solving, to be receptive to input from all areas, and to be flexible when change is required of you. When you must handle multiple demands, shifting priorities, and rapid-fire change, your best response is grounded in adaptability.

The key to mastering this factor is to know the difference between a reaction and a response. In stressful situations, we are more likely to react to individuals in a harsh, defensive, frustrated way. Any good manager is self-aware, knowing what he or she is feeling and why, and being able to take the time to breathe, think, and then respond to any situation shows that you have the ability to adapt, flex, and respect. Responding to situations moves you forward toward your goals; reacting slows you down, frustrates or humiliates your staff, and creates a level of negative visibility within the organization that lessens your credibility and value-adding status.

LEARNING

The best leaders understand that they do not know the answer to every question. For some leaders, the statement, "I don't know the answer to that question" is synonymous with saying, "I'm wrong; I should know." This right-wrong orientation to knowing versus learning may lead us to suppose that "knowing it all" is equivalent to being right and that needing to learn is a weakness that is somehow associated with being wrong.

In corporate America, a typical performance evaluation system will often support this right-wrong orientation to the knowing-learning continuum, effectively eliminating the opportunity to discover new ideas, learn new skills, and shift to behaviors that are more effective. If you must be seen as someone who knows everything, you are not going to gain knowledge from anyone else.

Managers who are committed to learning are more aware of their surroundings, are more receptive to ideas from others, conduct their work in order to more closely agree with their priorities and values, and allow the learning cycle to become the cornerstone of development for their organizations.

MANAGING FOR SUCCESS

Successful outsourcing managers have many traits and skills in common with expert managers around the world: they are accountable, responsible, trusting, and trustworthy; they focus on results rather than process; and they are able to handle (and defuse) difficult situations tactfully. They are adaptable to quick change; they give meaningful and timely feedback; and they welcome learning, both for themselves and for their staff. The main difference is the intensity of these traits—successful outsourcing managers must be better at all of them, and from a distance. Outsourcing managers who excel in these standard management practices can build teams that can collaborate across the miles, communicate clearly and often, and deliver outsourcing results that count.

CHAPTER 10

OUTSOURCING HURDLES AND HOW TO OVERCOME THEM

In addition to the outsourcing risks highlighted in Chapter 3, there are several significant hurdles that you may encounter on your way to outsourcing success. Most of the hurdles described here are related to an organizational focus on short-term gains rather than on achieving long-term success.

Geoff Smith, former deputy CIO of Procter & Gamble, points to a great example of the hurdles caused by the quick-win mentality: major-league baseball. Many major-league baseball teams neglected to invest in their minor-league farm systems, perhaps because of a short-term focus on saving money or because they traded their best young talent for hot-shot free agents who would help them achieve an immediate win. "In virtually every case," Smith says, "those pro teams went through prolonged bad times as they painstakingly rebuilt their talent base."

Poorly planned and implemented outsourcing programs are likely to produce similar problems and hurdles. Failing to notice potential ethical, educational, training, requirements definition, and other important agreement issues will slow your progress to a crawl. To overcome these challenges, review the following examples of the top hurdles you may encounter, along with advice on how to overcome them.

ETHICS

When outsourcing, particularly when outsourcing offshore, a new and significant issue involving the protection of sensitive or personal information emerges.

Take the case of a large national financial services organization that, unknowingly, engaged an outsourcing vendor with mob ties. Due to a lack of initial investigation of the outsource vendor and their employees and a lack of communication between the vendor and the organization, months passed before the organization realized their customer's confidential information was being sold to identity thieves.

So many things went wrong in this case that it is difficult to know where to start! One major contributor to this disaster was the vendor's IT director becoming aware of the problem, yet not disclosing it to anyone. If the organization had had an ongoing open communication program with its vendor, the vendor's IT director would have had a channel through which to disclose his awareness of the security breach immediately rather than waiting several months. If the vendor had been fully aware of the organization's privacy policy and its responsibilities related to the do-not-share clause, if the contract had required extensive background checks on employees, if the arrangement had included frequent site visits and ongoing management, if . . ., if . . ., if. . . .

Dr. Larry Ponemon of the Ponemon Institute recommends that organizations ask the following questions as a starting point to "practice safe outsourcing":

- Does the vendor have a published privacy policy, and does it limit data sharing?

- How adequate are the vendor's physical and electronic controls over data? Proof of controls would include self-certification such as an SAS 70. SAS 70, or Statement on Auditing Standards is an internationally recognized auditing standard developed by the American Institute of Certified Public Accountants (AICPA), representing that a service organization has been through an in-depth audit of their control activities, which generally include controls over information technology and related processes.

- Does the vendor have appropriate administrative controls in place?

- Does the vendor subcontract projects that use your data to other U.S. and non-U.S. vendors? If yes, are there control procedures in place, and are the procedures monitored?

- Does the vendor have a history of litigation or regulatory enforcement actions that pertain to privacy, data protection, or a general lack of compliance controls?

- Does the vendor permit you to independently verify the privacy and security procedures that are used to protect your company's data?

- Have you reviewed the vendor's S&P reports? If the vendor is a public company, have you reviewed its annual report and other financial filings?

- Does your vendor train employees to protect the data entrusted to them by your company?

- Are the vendor's senior executives willing to sign a pledge of compliance that states that the vendor will take all *reasonable* steps to comply with the terms of the contract and the privacy policy of your company?

- Is the vendor insured or does it have fidelity bonds to cover the possibility of a privacy or data security breach?

- Does the vendor have a live feed or online access to your company's data as part of the contractual requirement? If yes, is there some proof that access controls, identity management, and authentication are in place.

Dr. Ponemon is right: Not all vendor contracts are dependable. It is up to you to make sure that they are.

BRAIN DRAIN

By definition, brain drain occurs when a corporation becomes disconnected from its outsourcing service vendor while also failing to remain current with industry trends, standards, and developments. As a result, not only does the organization become operationally and strategically dependent on the outsourcing vendor, but a hole—an abyss—is created in the corporate knowledge base, a problem that becomes especially critical in the event that your exit strategy needs to be invoked.

Brain drain is actually knowledge loss, and we have experienced this over the years of expansion and contraction, downsizings and regrowth, and outsourcing and insourcing. Even given all of the history lessons available to us, organizations often fail to notice the problem of knowledge loss, at least until the damage is done and they are facing compromised business plans and growth strategies, reduced efficiency, and a marked decline in innovation.

Brain drain is a comprehensive problem associated with outsourcing, and one that requires a comprehensive solution. The real key is not to fix the problem of knowledge loss, but to prevent it in the first place through a focus on knowledge retention. Consider the following questions concerning knowledge retention in your organization:

- What knowledge is at risk as a result of your outsourcing initiative?

- Which current employees have the most critical knowledge?

- If your outsourcing initiative goes forward, what knowledge must you preserve in order to remain competitive, innovative, and on track with your business strategy?

- When your outsourcing initiative is in full force, what type of career development or succession planning must be established to maintain momentum?

- What education or training will current employees and employees in the new world order need in order for your organization to remain competitive over the next five to ten years?

- How many employees will be ready to retire over the next three to five years, and what can be done now to extend the tenure of the most valuable of these employees?

- Will your organization benefit from creating a mentor-contractor program in which seasoned, soon-to-be-retired executives serve as coaches and teachers for the new, young, just-out-of-school employees?

- Does your current company culture support knowledge retention in the form of wisdom and knowledge gained through experience?

Those companies that develop strategies to maintain their knowledge base understand the importance of education, training, and succession planning. Dick LeFave of Nextel asks, "Where are we going to find the CIOs of tomorrow?" To answer that question, Nextel implemented a college training program. Of the 350 college graduates who applied, 35 were interviewed, and 17 were hired to seed the entire organization with future knowledge brokers. The participants went through a six-week training program with coursework that included Web-based training, an executive lecture series, and site visits geared to exposing the college hires not only to the IT function at Nextel, but to how the department affects the entire organization. Mentoring was also a cornerstone of the program, providing veteran IT staffers with a chance to give back to the youth in their field and contribute to the positive growth of the function.

To avoid brain drain in your organization, review your business strategy in an effort to create a solution that sticks. If, as most companies find, the main problem area is culture, get a culture shift started immediately (see Chapter 15 for resources on coaching and culture change). There is never a good time to lose key sources of competitive advantage; avoid the loss by addressing the brain drain/knowledge retention issue up front.

SALESPEOPLE VERSUS EXECUTIVES

When a sales consultant for an outsourcing service provider makes big, shiny promises, those promises are difficult to ignore. Clever consultants may sway you with reports of their impressive leverage with vendors, extensive experience and knowledge base, superior staff, and outstanding tools and systems—if you will only trust them, they can do what you do better, faster, and for less money. An unaware executive might be tempted to sign on the dotted line before completing a competitive RFP process, due diligence, or reference checks. This problem is called *sales versus executives*.

In any industry, a good salesperson's goal is to get the executive to purchase the product being sold. An outsourcing initiative can be an exciting, big project that can be very attractive to an executive whose job it is to improve shareholder value—when the persuasive salesperson meets the executive who wants to make a big impact, who could say no?

Be wary of sales representatives for outsourcing firms who are unclear about your needs, your problems, or your business plan and are focused on getting a signature on a contract. If their approach is to push you ("sign today and I'll give you a significant discount"), show them the door. If their approach is "given enough time and money, we will eventually get what you need," it is time to run. Purchasing a one-size-fits-all outsourcing program is doomed to failure.

Every outsourcing initiative must include a competitive bidding process, a comprehensive due-diligence process, and a test drive. Quick decisions line the path to outsourcing hell.

SCOPE CREEP

Scope creep is an expression used by organizations that find that they need their vendors to deliver work in excess of what was originally agreed upon. Scope creep typically results from a failure to establish clear requirements definitions, so that the scope of the work begins to increase.

Some outsourcing professionals suggest that scope creep is simply a way for an organization to become clear about what it really wants from the vendor. This is a dangerous formula on which to base your relationship.

When an outsourcing vendor submits a proposal, it describes in general terms what it is going to do. It rarely provides a detailed description of how things will work and who will do what, when, and how well. Developing a document that is explicit takes a great deal of time and effort (see Chapters 4 and 5 for more information on this), and it requires the cooperation of senior management and the people whose positions may soon be eliminated.

When scope creep begins, the organization and the vendor usually have a different idea of what needs to be done, by whom, and when. For example, the organization assumes that the vendor will complete every job function that its recently displaced W-2 employees carried out. The vendor, on the other hand, assumes that it has defined the functions that it will perform, the components of which are far fewer than the work the displaced W-2 employees performed, and the vendor believes that it has priced the services based on this premise.

When you have poorly defined requirements combined with a weak and ambivalent proposal, you end up with an unhappy relationship and an outsourcing initiative that is fated to fail. The fix for this is easy: Define your requirements, manage your relationship, monitor your progress, report on a regular basis, and communicate as often as possible.

PHILOSOPHICAL DIFFERENCES

Often dissatisfaction with an outsourcing engagement is based on a failure to design a relationship that will work for both parties. Organizations meticulously create solid foundations for their customer relationships, and the same type of painstaking relationship design process must take place with your vendor.

The organization often has unspoken expectations that the vendor will behave exactly the way the organization's W-2 staff behaved. For example, an organization may ask an exempt W-2 employee to handle additional work on a special project. A professional, exempt W-2 employee will reset her or his priorities and complete the extra work. Assuming that your vendor will handle a special project outside of the specific requirements definitions is unrealistic—the vendor has charged a defined price for a defined scope of work. Extra work equals scope creep.

If these issues are not defined during the contract phase, the organization will continue to ask for extra work, the vendor will continue to ask for more money, and the organization will begin to believe that the vendor is gouging it, leading to the deterioration of the relationship.

CUSTOMER SATISFACTION

When the focus of an outsourcing initiative is entirely on cost reduction, organizations can lose sight of why they are in business in the first place: serving their customers. If your outsourcing program is not looked at through your customers' eyes, your customers may walk out, making any cost savings seem trivial.

The organization's focus on cost savings in the example of the customer call center outsourced to India (see Chapter 4) is clear. The failure cycle began when the organization did not communicate to the vendor that 90 percent of its customers were Spanish-speaking, and the vendor failed to recognize that its staff was unable to speak Spanish. A colossal and costly mistake, this outsourcing blunder is likely to cause far-reaching customer service difficulties for the financial services organization for some time to come.

Successful outsourcing requires so much up-front work because there are so many entities involved: your customers, employees, and shareholders; the vendor; and your organization. Take the time, with the right team of people, to look at your outsourcing program through the eyes of your customer.

SCALABILITY

The issue of scalability incorporates how well your outsourcing program will work when the size of your business increases. Scalability is often used only in the programming or high-tech world, yet when it comes to outsourcing, the issue of scalability applies to every situation. If your vendor offers appropriate scalability, it is offering to expand or increase its capabilities as your organization requires—it has the ability to grow with your needs. For example, if your vendor will be providing a scalable call center program, you will be able to use only the resources you need now, with the ability to grow by expanding your vendor's staff when your circumstances warrant it. If the scalability issue is addressed up front, the expansion of scale can be quite simple. If the scalability issue is overlooked, the expansion of scale looks a lot like scope creep.

Outsourcing programs must be positioned to meet your growth requirements, and if this is not considered during the vendor-selection phase, it can present a major hurdle once your program starts to show some progress. Look beyond a vendor's current capabilities; focus on its scale.

EXECUTIVE BUY-IN

Executive buy-in and support must drive the outsourcing initiative in order for it to be successful. In fact, the biggest obstacle to implementing an outsourcing initiative is the internal resistance within the corporation, and that resistance is often at the top of the organization.

While a change management program helps in managing that resistance, a successful outsourcing initiative requires enthusiastic support and active involvement by the senior leadership. In researching this book, I found that when an outsourcing initiative fails, lack of executive sponsorship is always a key factor.

Mike Matteo of 360Sourcing.com reveals one of the things he has witnessed that can lead you to success or failure. "The first thing," Matteo suggests, "is executive sponsorship. When a VP level tries to act on his own without senior-level support, the program will come to a screeching halt because there is no senior buy-in." Executives must get involved, ask questions, show support, and help others in the organization move forward with the changes. Without that demonstration of executive support, the entire organization will demonstrate resistance, too.

If the executive level does not buy into an outsourcing initiative before the contract is signed, there is trouble ahead.

Before implementing an outsourcing initiative, organizations must be aware of the hazards and hurdles, and must commit to completing a study of those potential pitfalls before signing on the dotted line. The hidden costs, the potential ethical dilemmas, scope creep, scalability, philosophical differences, and customer satisfaction issues all must be considered carefully before executing an outsourcing contract. Successful outsourcing initiatives are successful because these obstacles have been evaluated, so make the time to investigate all of these issues—then review, monitor, and test to make sure that your initiative is on, and stays on, the right track.

CHAPTER 11

DEALING WITH CULTURAL AND LANGUAGE BARRIERS

The legend of General Motors' introduction of its Chevy Nova into the Latin American market in the 1980s is a perfect example of differences in culture. As the story goes, GM introduced the Chevy Nova into Latin markets before first investigating the translation of the word *Nova*. In Spanish, the word *Nova* or *no va*, is literally translated as "it does not go." Parable or truth, this story certainly makes a point about culture.

In today's economic climate, organizations do not have time to make mistakes, and initiating an outsourcing engagement that fails is an expensive mistake. Working effectively on any outsourcing initiative, onshore or off, requires a broad understanding of and sensitivity to cultural differences in order to achieve success. This culturally aware approach to outsourcing demands knowledge, insight, and skill, along with mastery of the ability to recognize the expectations and style of your vendor. To be culturally aware opens the door to communication of critical information early and clearly, so that organizations and their outsourcing vendors can be more effective managers, avoiding misunderstandings or offending others, and building relationships that are critical to success.

Cultural issues may be one of the most commonly overlooked and misunderstood barriers to successful outsourcing. Let's face it, trying to communicate the details of a project across the country can be tricky, depending on who is sending the information and who is receiving the information. Take that same communication across the continents, and you have a formula for confusion and misunderstanding.

As the Chinese proverb says, "Dig the well before you are thirsty." Intelligent outsourcing initiatives identify and prepare for the culture gap early in the process. Some of the differences encountered will be based on things like values and customs, some differences will be based on language, and some differences will be based on geography. The key here is to avoid those costly missteps that lead to lost time, lost money, or your invoking your exit strategy. Three of the most prevalent cultural issues are highlighted here: time, language, and culture.

TIME

Depending on the country and the location, time differences can affect service in mild to extreme ways. For example, when I am working with clients across the United States, I attempt to make the three-hour California–New York time difference work in our favor—some executives prefer to work with their coach after hours, and 6 p.m. Eastern time is 3 p.m. Pacific time, so it works for both of us. Sometimes, though, that time difference is a burden.

The headquarters of a financial services organization, located in Connecticut, begins its workday at 9 a.m. Eastern time. The organization's California office begins work at 9 a.m. Pacific time, or noon Eastern time—just about the time the Connecticut people are headed out to lunch. The East Coast people return from lunch around 1 p.m. Eastern time (10 a.m. Pacific time), leaving approximately a two-hour window in which to conduct any real-time communications prior to the West Coasters' lunch hour. When the California people return to work at 1 p.m. Pacific time, it is now 4 p.m. Eastern time, leaving an opportunity for approximately one additional hour of real-time communication. In short, between the two U.S. coasts, there are approximately three hours per day when staff members can actually speak with one another.

Let's move that example to include the span between California and India. There is a 13½-hour time difference; in a typical office situation, there will not be any period during which synchronized communication between these two locations is possible. With the amount of communication that is required between organization and vendor, this time gap can create a considerable problem.

Gina Dias, corporate controller for Network Video Technologies in California, knows firsthand the problems of managing staff and programs across the globe. With locations in London (plus 8 hours), Singapore (plus 14 hours), Pennsylvania (plus 3 hours), and Mexico (plus 2 hours), Dias has had her hands full scheduling all-hands meetings, staff briefings, and feedback sessions. Knowing the importance of communicating, the regularly scheduled 4 a.m. Pacific time meetings are not delegated; she leads each one from her home office.

WHAT CAN YOU DO TO ACCOMMODATE TIME-ZONE DIFFERENCES?

Depending on the country and the location, time differences are likely to affect your vendor relationship in some way. Real-time meetings can be a challenge given the time-zone differences, yet making them work in your favor is possible. To accommodate the time-zone differences, consider the following ideas:

• Schedule meetings as far ahead as possible to allow people to adjust their schedules.

• When between the in-house and outsourced teams have to be coordinated, one group is probably going to be inconvenienced; they will either have to stay several hours late or come in several hours early. One way to reinforce the team concept, partnership model, and relationship development is to rotate the timing of the conference calls or meetings so that each group takes a turn at being inconvenienced.

• Plan for your in-house staff to shift their work hours or occasionally be "on call." If someone from across the country or across the world has a problem or question that requires a response from your organization, that vendor's work will most likely stop until the vendor receives your directions.

• Set up a "hot line" that lets your vendor reach you during *your* working hours, in case serious issues arise.

Other methods for dealing with time differences are highlighted in Chapter 9, such as online message boards, blogging, instant messaging, Web sites for posting reports and results, e-mail, and voice mail.

Organizations can learn how to take advantage of the time differences between locations to sustain healthy relationships, improve communications, and solve problems. To use the time differences effectively, organizations must create a well-defined communication plan to ensure that there is a consistency in the understanding of requirements, effective project management in multiple locations, and ample coordination between the vendor and the organization.

LANGUAGE

Linguists estimate that there are between five and six thousand different languages spoken in the world today. Even though the English language is only the third most common language in the world (behind Mandarin Chinese and Hindi as numbers one and two, respectively), it is, as you might expect, far more worldwide in its distribution than all other spoken languages.

Part of the problem with language in outsourcing is that English is not always the same. The differences among American dialects across the United States are astounding; add the differences in English around the world, and the results can range from humorous to offensive.

Even though the use of English is widespread, it is not a primary language in many countries, so when you are outsourcing offshore, it is important to identify a primary language for written and verbal communications. When completing your vendor-selection process, a best practice is to identify the English language and dialect capabilities of your offshore vendor, while also having a number of in-house employees who are fluent in the language of the vendor's country.

With over 20 years of experience in outsourcing on- and offshore, Art Salyer of Trojan Batteries is not comfortable with an outsourcing initiative if he does not speak the vendor's language. Over the years, he has become proficient in Japanese, Chinese, Portuguese, and Spanish to communicate in the languages native to his outsourcing providers. "Build language into your transfer of work," Salyer says. "Use language immersion courses with refresher classes until you and your staff can speak the language to communicate with your vendor. It makes all the difference."

Consider offering cultural and language cross training to your team and your vendor contacts to make sure that you are literally speaking the same language. Companies have offered cross-cultural and language training for many years for the purpose of international relocation preparation; the same type of training is now offered by companies with a focus on building partnerships while removing language and culture as a barrier.

When you are working with a customer service program offshore—a call center, for example—it is vitally important that the offshore staff become cognizant of the differences in language and style between call center employees and their American customers. Call center employees are an extension of your organization and, as such, a major part of your brand. It is worth your time and effort to ensure that your offshore call center employees speak superb English; anything less than superb call center staff will be more likely to stick to a precise script when answering customer calls, and will be unable to fully engage in discussion of the customers' issues. Without open conversation, many customers will become frustrated and conclude that the call center employee is, in the words of an executive I know, "courteous and ineffective."

Remember, too, that the opportunities for cost savings that may be available in an offshore customer-related outsourcing program are inconsequential in the face of declining customer satisfaction rates.

CULTURE

"When you outsource offshore, no matter what, it is their country. Forcing a U.S. management style is a recipe for disaster."
—ART SALYER, EVP OF OPERATIONS, TROJAN BATTERY COMPANY

Webster's defines *culture* as "the shared beliefs, customs, practices, and social behavior of a particular nation or people." In the real world, however, a specific definition of culture is difficult to produce because the characteristics we use to refer to cultural differences are not universally applicable—in fact, they are quite subjective. Global differences in attitudes and approaches to work and working relationships in different countries and regions must be identified and clarified during the outsourcing planning process; for example,

• Brian Maloney, former COO of Perot Systems, identifies cultural and style differences as a constraint in offshore outsourcing. "The cultural differences are the biggest problems—it's the way people deal with people," Maloney states. "In certain cultures, people are very agreeable, and want to make a good impression. The problem is, they may say 'yes' when they really mean 'no,' an obvious setup for misunderstandings." This yes-no behavior leads to increased expectations of service or results on the U.S. side, with shame and fear on the vendor side.

- Scott Nobel, director of Global Sourcing Insights, advises companies on offshore outsourcing as a business strategy. Nobel's white paper entitled "Why Offshore Outsourcing Projects Fail" (see Chapter 15 to obtain a copy) hits the cultural nail right on the head. For example, Nobel states, "In some Latin cultures, work is not the defining entity in one's life to the extent that we commonly find in the United States. This can lead to a more casual approach to schedules that can exasperate U.S. businesspeople." This particular difference in style and culture may be perceived from a U.S. standpoint as a lack of a sense of urgency. Latin cultures tend to see the "American preoccupation with clock-watching and strict adherence to schedules to be obsessive." Latin cultures do have a sense of urgency, quality, and productivity—however stylistically different from the U.S. perspective it may be. U.S. organizations must identify and clarify the definitions of "urgency, quality, and productivity" so that the vendor and the organization understand each other.

- E-mail is a formal method of communication here in the United States, yet it is often considered disrespectful and impersonal in countries like Malaysia and South Korea. U.S. organizations working in the global arena must identify the best ways to communicate with their vendors, not just from a technical perspective, but from a cultural perspective as well. If e-mail is considered disrespectful, organizations must consider other modes of communication that will foster trust and commitment between the vendor and the organization.

- Nobel also shares his experience with cultural differences between Asia and the United States. In some Asian cultures, "there is a fundamental deference to and respect for author-ity figures that can cause some personnel from these cul-tures to not question work assignments in the same way we have come to expect from U.S. employees," Nobel says. In the United States, we expect our employees to question assignments to make sure that they understand the desired outcomes and the most effective ways of achieving those outcomes. In certain Asian cultures, however, the respect factor may keep the vendor's employees from questioning work assignments, desired outcomes, and most effective ways to accomplish the desired results. Rather, in this cul-tural style, the vendor's employees may go directly to work on the assignment as written, without question (even if they have a recommendation for improvement).

The key here, Nobel recommends, is to establish an appropriate means of communication, technologically and culturally. "Find a means by which you can obtain feedback without breaching cultural protocol." Focus on data exchange rather than the person; make it easy to create the give and take required to succeed.

Oddly, one of the biggest contributors to poor commu-nication is actually lack of communication. Beyond lan-guage, timing, and cultural issues, when access to information is limited, it is a precursor to disaster. A lack of information flow from organization to vendor may seem to imply indifference: The vendor assumes that the organization does not care. Informing staff on both sides of the spectrum, asking for input, revealing changes in roles and responsibilities, and giving and receiving feed-back are important parts of any communication program, and when shared early and often, they will help to build the relationships required to make this entire outsourcing program worthwhile.

STATUS AND CULTURAL DIFFERENCES

All societies and cultures seem to bestow status on individuals in one way or another. In U.S. corporations, the hierarchical system consists of many layers and levels: A CEO has a more privileged status level than a file clerk. The hierarchical systems of countries and cultures outside of the U.S. corporate system may be more difficult to comprehend because the characteristics used to measure status can vary considerably from one culture to another.

ASCRIBED-STATUS CULTURES

In some cultures, an individual's status is founded on external qualities, such as age, gender, or social class. In an ascribed-status culture, an individual with a 20-year employment history will be granted more respect than a new young hotshot, regardless of the hotshot's contribution to the company. For example, Scott Nobel related that in his experience working with Indian national employees, status is based on social class. "Depending on your position, you may not have the status level required to speak to all employees. This means important conversations *will not happen.*" Individuals with the "right" external qualities are given the highest status and hold the highest positions, professionally and socially.

ACHIEVED-STATUS CULTURES

Achieved-status cultures tend to value accomplishments rather than age or social standing. A new young hotshot has as much or more status in an organization than an average performing employee with 20 years of experience with the company. In these cultures, forward progression into positions of power and influence is granted by virtue of your achievements and performance rather than being a function of birth, age, or seniority. This type of status is earned, and it can be forfeited if your achievements wane.

CHAIN OF COMMAND:
ASCRIBED-STATUS CULTURES

Vendors with internal social structure systems that are heavily influenced by an ascribed-status culture tend to be more rigid in defining the roles and responsibilities of employees based on their status. Employees, therefore, focus only on tasks that fall within their specific job responsibility, as they may not believe themselves empowered to make recommendations for improvement to those identified as their superiors. In an ascribed-status culture, changes or improvements will be made only when they are presented *to* the right person, at the right level, *by* the right person.

Dealing with different cultures can be tricky. To communicate well with your outsourcing vendor, you must become familiar with diverse styles, become fluent in different languages, learn and respect different traditions, and respect the vendor's view of status.

So much of your outsourcing success is based on communication—and the cultural/language topic is no exception. Communication equals success.

U.S. organizations outsourcing offshore must create communication methods that respect the vendor's culture and class system, yet open communication so that results can be achieved. Address the issues of communication, language, culture, and status during the vendor-selection process so that the proper protocols can be established early; with careful planning, communication, and cultural sensitivity, you can reduce the bumps in this road to globalization.

PART 4

THE BALANCING ACT

At this point in your evaluation process, you know that a properly planned and efficiently managed outsourcing program can enhance productivity, decrease costs, and improve quality. Yet there is a paradox created in any outsourcing situation when attempting to balance the short-term and long-terms needs of shareholders, vendors, managers, and customers. The key is to create sustainable shareholder value without sacrificing quality, productivity, relationships, or control.

Another part of the balancing act is knowing when, and how, to pull the plug on an outsourcing engagement that just is not working. Developing an effective exit strategy requires up-front discussions with your vendor, and the implementation of an exit strategy that leaves you whole requires a close and continuous legal overview.

The following chapters address the balancing act with all stakeholders, and what to do when the party is over.

CHAPTER 12

BALANCING THE NEEDS

When outsourcing, organizations must strike a delicate balance among all stakeholders: employees, vendors, customers, and shareholders. Developing and maintaining this balance can be difficult when you are attempting to identify and control the present and future expectations and strategies of all involved parties. To generate sustainable shareholder value without sacrificing quality, productivity, relationships, key employees, or control, this delicate balance must be addressed as directly and urgently as if it were another product or service offering.

One of the most widely debated issues today is the dichotomy between the different views of the organization's responsibilities to its numerous stakeholders. At one extreme, senior managers and boards of directors are seen as being responsible only to the shareholders, and at the other extreme, senior managers and boards of directors are seen as being responsible to a wide array of stakeholders. The former position argues that organizations have but one responsibility: to maximize shareholder wealth. The latter argues that organizations have a responsibility to a broader constituency than only shareholders, including customers, vendors, employees, and the community.

For your outsourcing initiative to be successful, the long-term approach to value is a best practice. To envision the issue as a whole, consider that you are looking at a table with four legs. Each leg represents a different aspect of the support system for the success of your outsourcing initiative: One leg represents shareholder value, one leg represents employee value, one leg represents vendor value, and one leg represents customer value. Your goal is to maintain an equal balance for each of those table legs—and if you spend too much time and attention on any one of the table legs, that leg will continue to grow while the other legs will begin to shrink. Organizations whose center of attention is shareholder value, for example, lose the balance with the other equally important components of the process, and the table quickly falls over.

To find the requisite balance, organizations must manage the expectations of each entity: shareholders, employees, vendors, and customers. Before managing these expectations, however, a common understanding of value for each stakeholder group must be defined.

SHAREHOLDER VALUE

In today's world of unpredictable markets, erratic investors, and increasing global competition, there is extreme pressure on companies to deliver profitable growth and a healthy return to investors. While the goal of every for-profit organization is to find the right business strategies and investments to consistently grow the company's profitability, quantifying shareholder value creation is often a challenge.

Several philosophies exist with respect to how organizations define the process of shareholder value creation. We know that maximizing shareholder value is a major objective, yet we also know that a singular focus on shareholder value, especially short-term value, may leave the other stakeholders out in the cold.

For example, "If shareholder value is based only on near-term stock prices, you may be on the road to failure," says Scott Nobel of Global Source Insights.

> We have historically measured executive performance by shareholder value, and we have historically measured shareholder value by near-term stock price. Take the massive layoffs in the 1980s—companies would lay off 10,000 people today, knowing they would have to rehire 6,000 people next year. However, if they lay off those 10,000 people today, the stock price goes up today, and the executive performance, measured by shareholder value, measured by stock price, is increased. This near-term stock price increase is not in fact added shareholder value, because in the long term those layoffs cost millions of dollars, eliminating any long-term growth.

Value-creating organizations make decisions that maintain a suitable balance among the competing interests of all stakeholders; organizations that create long-term shareholder value simultaneously create relatively greater value for all stakeholders. Consequently, value-creating organizations operate with a primary objective of maximizing shareholder value, while also working to satisfy the requirements of the remaining stakeholders.

Using an outsourcing initiative to create greater shareholder value must have a long-term strategic purpose; this may require making a less aggressive entry into the outsourcing arena and may involve sacrificing some short-term gains in favor of long-term growth. Outsourcing, when properly planned and implemented, adds to shareholder value when

- The projected cost savings are sustainable in the long term.

- Key staff is retained.

- Customers are not affected.

- Quality is not diminished.

- Service is not compromised.

In outsourcing, shareholder value is driven by much more than near-term stock prices. Effective and efficient outsourcing initiatives provide for sustainable shareholder value that will increase in the long term with a more profitable company.

EMPLOYEE VALUE

To create employee value, an organization must make its business a place where people feel valued, want to work, and do not want to leave. This may sound simplistic, but when the pressures of implementing an outsourcing initiative become the main event, management's concentration tends to be directed exclusively toward getting through the execution process, leaving little time and attention for the employee base. Considering that the proper implementation of a successful outsourcing initiative can take several months to two years, the opportunity for the loss of human capital is even greater during this period.

In general, people want opportunities to grow in their jobs—to advance in position, opportunity, responsibility, and compensation. Employees go to work to be recognized for their contributions and accomplishments, to be respected as individuals, and to be intellectually stimulated.

To create an environment in which key people will stay and produce the results you want, you need to use incentive programs for your employees and to keep your employees well informed at every stage of your outsourcing initiative; rather than making presentations to update employees, create an open dialogue where they can discuss and question what is really going on. Understand their perspective, and shift and change your approach accordingly. Make the time to let employees know that you value their input, and you will reap the rewards of increased focus; reduced absenteeism; heightened morale; improved productivity; increased and improved communications internally, with vendors, and with customers; and reduced costs of hiring and training new employees.

Remember, employee value leads to vendor value, which leads to customer value, which leads to shareholder value.

VENDOR VALUE

Outsourcing vendors want your business; good outsourcing vendors want your business long-term. They want to make it easy for you to work with them; they want to know what you want; they want to deliver what you need; and they want to communicate with you often.

Lilia Tsalalikhin is vice president and chief marketing officer of Luxoft, a software development vendor based in

Moscow, Russia (and with numerous offices in the United States and Europe). As she puts it,

> We are recognized as a service provider who makes the entire process simple for our clients. We want to make the transition of work fast, easy, and complete, and we want to deliver on the business and financial goals of our clients. The outsourcing industry used to focus only on cost of labor as a metric for calculating success; we focus on the return on outsourcing (ROO) for our clients. Our success is our client's success.

True value for a vendor is in its maintaining you as a client. It is far less expensive for the vendor to retain the clients it has than to go out and sign a new client, and it is far less expensive for the organization to find the right vendor and work together than to invoke an exit strategy and start over with another RFP process. Work to create an open dialogue with your vendor so that the vendor completely understands your perspective and expectations; check for understanding so that you are clear that the vendor knows what you want.

Developing and maintaining these vendor relationships takes work—as does developing and maintaining any other relationship. Work to create and sustain the vendor value proposition in order to deliver customer value, which leads to shareholder value.

CUSTOMER VALUE

What is required to deliver customer satisfaction during an outsourcing implementation? Predictability: Customers want to know that they will receive the same (or better) levels of service, product, delivery, and so on as they had experienced prior to your transition to an outsourcing vendor.

Customer satisfaction is a tricky thing. Some customers are satisfied with the service or product you deliver, so much so that they are loyal to your sales or service representatives as well as to your organization. Truly satisfied and loyal customers will flex with you as you make the transition to your outsourcing program.

Some customers, however, may report a low to moderate level of satisfaction in response to your service evaluations even when they are completely dissatisfied. With this group, any change, especially a change in contact, service, products, quality, communication frequency, or the "no surprises" customer service approach, will create hurdles that are difficult to overcome. These less-than-satisfied customers are the most volatile—their loyalty level may not create the patience and flexibility that are required during an outsourcing transition.

In order to sustain or improve customer satisfaction and loyalty during this process, you must first identify the service satisfaction and loyalty levels of your current customers. This assessment becomes the standard by which you develop and maintain your customers' perception of value in your outsourcing program. With these benchmark data in hand, work with your service provider to include a customer satisfaction and loyalty analysis as part of the key performance indicators in your outsourcing contract. This satisfaction and loyalty assessment will provide another meaningful measurement of service for your vendor, will be based on established customer expectations, and will help you focus on maintaining the customers you already have. It is customer satisfaction that, when managed properly, leads to customer loyalty, and customer loyalty adds to shareholder value.

MANAGING EXPECTATIONS

Let's recap: Customer loyalty is driven by customer satisfaction, which is driven by employee value and vendor value, which leads to shareholder value. Each of these stakeholders comes to this party with a separate agenda and separate expectations. Customers expect to receive excellent service (or products), vendors expect to be your partners (long-term), employees expect to be valued and rewarded, and stockholders expect your outsourcing initiative to make money. These expectations are visions of a future state or action, are usually *unspoken*, and are critical to your success.

"Expectations aren't set one time; they are continuously in a state of flux. A discussion by the coffee machine, a recently read article, or a meeting with a vendor can all serve to change what stakeholders expect," says George Spafford of Spafford Consulting. Because expectations are dynamic by nature, they require a continuous management process, beginning with regular communications with each party to understand and manage that party's expectations.

1. *Shape the expectations.* Expectations become more firmly cast in stone the longer they are ignored. Addressing expectations early allows you to mold and set the expectations of each stakeholder. Conduct an expectation meeting early in your outsourcing process. Well before the contract is signed, meet with each stakeholder group to identify what it thinks *should* happen, and carefully address anything that is unrealistic or inaccurate. Work toward a combined and balanced set of initial expectations, commit these expectations to writing, and decide how often updates, or true-ups, should be held. (*Note:* Waiting until after the contract is signed to hold these

expectation meetings may cause vendor performance issues or scope creep.)

2. *Monitor.* You cannot manage what you do not measure, and you cannot manage stakeholder expectations unless you monitor them closely. Customer service and loyalty, employee performance and satisfaction, vendor performance and relationship management, and shareholder satisfaction can be monitored, managed, and reported. Create an appropriate process for each entity (targets, surveys, and so on) based on that stakeholder's expectations, carefully monitor progress, and report back to each entity.

3. *Report.* Since expectations are dynamic, regular reporting of progress is required. Circle back with each stakeholder group to review the initial expectations, report on progress, and set new criteria for expectations for the next period. During these meetings, take advantage of the opportunity to build credibility, establish trust, educate, and influence the next set of expectations.

SUMMARY

When balancing the needs of all stakeholders, think in the long term. The main road to shareholder value is through executive leadership that drives the support system that achieves long-term value through operational excellence (in-house and outsourced), product and service quality, and, of course, customer intimacy.

CHAPTER 13

EXIT MANAGEMENT

When an outsourcing engagement fails, a good contract with clearly outlined exit provisions will save time and money—and perhaps save the entire outsourcing initiative. In the following real (but anonymous) examples shared by outsourcing attorney and expert Brad Peterson, the cause of the outsourcing failures and the subsequent exit problems teach us what happens when you are unprepared for exit management, and what can happen when you are completely prepared for exit management.

EXAMPLE 1

A vendor's sales team promised a product that the vendor's operations team could not implement. When contracted delivery dates were missed, the vendor was found to be in material breach of contract, and the organization terminated under the "for cause" provision of its outsourcing contract. That was the good news; the bad news was that the contract transition-out costs were about one-third of the costs of beginning the outsourcing program, and the additional costs of making the transition to a new vendor were another one-third of the original costs of the outsourcing contract. The cost of resolving a troubled contract is between one-half and five times the cost of entering into the contract, depending on how well your exit provisions are written.

EXAMPLE 2

An organization rushed to sign an outsourcing contract to meet stock market expectations for cost savings. Unfortunately, the outsourcing deal structure (pricing) was wrong for the organization, and the cost savings were not there—and neither was any form of exit provisions. Shortly after the implementation of the outsourcing program, the organization moved to terminate the contract, stating that the vendor had wasted time and money and was not delivering on the results requirements. The vendor, hoping to avoid termination, hired its own attorney and suggested that the organization had neglected to provide adequate background information to enable the vendor to deliver results. While the case was before the court, the organization assessed what had made this deal go south: It had rushed to sign a contract without thinking it through. In an effort to move quickly to satisfy Wall Street, it had gone ahead without having a clear idea of what it had purchased, how much it was going to cost, or how it could manage its exit if necessary. As a result, the organization lost time, key in-house employees, money, credibility with Wall Street, and customers.

EXAMPLE 3

An organization outsourced a call center for technical support of its computer hardware products. The contract was well defined, with service-level agreements, benchmarks for performance, and exit provisions. The goal was for the vendor to receive positive customer service responses for "satisfied call resolution" of 80 percent. After several months, the organization found that the call resolution rate was 36 percent, and customers were getting angry. The organization reviewed its contract, found the vendor to be in material violation of the service requirements, and issued a preliminary termination notice to the vendor.

The vendor's first response was to abdicate responsibility because it believed that the organization had not provided proper training, adequate scripts for the call center employees, or a comprehensive description of the types of calls the outsourcing center would be responsible for answering.

Rather than pulling the entire contract, the organization routed to the vendor only those calls that were similar to the 36 percent that it handled well; the remaining calls were routed to an engineering call center in-house. To maintain contract minimums, the organization committed to sending additional work to the vendor, and the outsourcing engagement remains profitable for both vendor and organization.

LEAVING A RELATIONSHIP

When you reach the executive level in corporate America, most career and legal experts would advise you to negotiate a comprehensive employment contract. The typical employment contract covers position, duties, responsibilities, goals, length of assignment, compensation, bonuses—and, of course, exit terms. These exit terms clarify under what conditions the employment contract may be terminated, and what will happen with respect to benefits, compensation, bonuses, vacation, severance, stock options, and so on if the contract is terminated. For some executives, it is difficult to consider negotiating a departure strategy prior to beginning a new assignment, but experience proves that the best time to agree on exit arrangements is before your employment contract is signed.

Once vendor decisions have been made, there is a tendency on both sides (organization and vendor) to speak of the future only in positive terms. While discussing how well they and the vendor will work together, opportunities for growth, and optimistic visions of the future, organizations may neglect to discuss the circumstances under which they may want or need to invoke an exit strategy. Discussions of the finer points of bailing out may not be comfortable at this joyous point in the process, yet having a bailout plan is crucial to your success.

Brad Peterson, our outsourcing legal expert, agrees that the development of exit management provisions is not an assignment for a novice. "These termination provisions require thought because they may be unique to your business and because you cannot expect to find them in a service provider's template contract," Peterson says. Producing legally binding yet flexible exit provisions, all of which will also work well in practice alongside other provisions of the contract, is a complex challenge at best. Some simple but fundamental questions must be addressed, including these:

- Who can terminate the outsourcing contract, when can it be terminated, and under what circumstances?

- Who owns what related to the work completed, and how will this change?

- How will the transition of the work to the new vendor or back in-house be accomplished, by whom, and when?

- How, and by whom, will the service be delivered in the future?

• How much will this cost, and who will be responsible for payment?

Addressing these initial questions during due diligence gives the organization a huge advantage. Allow each vendor bidding on your project to commit to your exit requirements, and build the exit terms and conditions into your original outsourcing contract. Dealing with your exit strategy up front may limit the vendor's ability to give you a rock-bottom price, so the negotiation of these points requires a delicate balance. By the time you have signed your outsourcing contract, these exit management elements are fixed; if the exit strategy must be invoked, the specifics of who, what, how, when, and how much have been predetermined, and the approach to the transition will be streamlined.

LOCKED IN

If you have ever experienced a dependent vendor relationship, you are familiar with being "locked in." For example, if a single bank provides your checking, savings, merchant, credit card, and investment accounts, but delivers poor customer service, you may postpone moving all of your financial accounts to another bank simply because it is too difficult and time-consuming to do so. You are locked in.

Similar circumstances can occur with your outsourcing vendor. This locked-in situation is a lopsided contractual arrangement in which organizations choose to continue to work with a vendor, even if the vendor's work is substandard, simply because it is too difficult to get out of the contract. When exit provisions are not included in the initial negotiation for vendor services, organizations may disregard the poor performance of their vendors because they feel trapped. The locked-in situation may be real or perceived, and it may be based on financial issues (the fees associated with changing vendors are exorbitant), operational issues (the service disruption to the client would be devastating), or simply a nuisance factor (the time and energy required to begin the entire outsourcing process again can be staggering). In any event, being at the mercy of your outsourcing vendor is bad business and completely avoidable.

In addition to considering why and how you would manage your exit from a vendor contract, organizations must also consider their next steps. Depending on the circumstances, there are several paths to consider as next steps, including the following:

• Renegotiate your current contract with your existing vendor.

• Procure a new vendor (develop a new RFP, conduct due diligence, select a vendor, test the arrangement, contract with the new vendor, train staff, and transfer the work).

• Bring the service/product back in-house.

To be complete in your initial outsourcing contract negotiations is to consider the factors of why you would want to exit, how you would accomplish the exit, and how you will handle business, clients, employees, and shareholders after the exit.

WHY EXIT?

Just as employment contracts provide "for cause" and "at will" exit provisions, best-practice outsourcing agreements include "for-cause" and "for-convenience" exit provisions.

A for-cause exit provision involves a breach of the contract, while a for-convenience provision is similar to an at-will provision (either party may exit for any reason or no reason at all). With the former provision, exit is generally permitted without fee; with the latter, a substantial "termination for-convenience fee" is generally negotiated.

What happens if your vendor goes out of business, fails to meet its financial agreements, underperforms, files for bankruptcy, or is simply unable to keep pace with the innovations in your market? If any of these events occurs, and you must terminate your contract with your vendor, how do you plan to manage your exit to limit the effect on your customers, employees, senior management, and shareholders?

FOR CAUSE OR CONVENIENCE

Peterson recommends that organizations consider all circumstances under which they might want to terminate the contract for cause or convenience. Events such as a material breach of contract, failure to achieve specific milestones, and ongoing failure to achieve predetermined service levels are some of the typical reasons to terminate for cause. Peterson recommends that organizations consider additional circumstances permitting termination, such as

- Force majeure events (failure to perform contractual obligations caused by unavoidable events beyond the vendor's control, such as natural disasters or wars)

- Changes in tax laws or other external circumstances

- Significant organizational business changes (merger, acquisition, bankruptcy)

- Significant vendor business changes (change in control of vendor, acquisition of vendor by a competitor of the customer; insolvency)

- Pre-insolvency conditions, such as dramatic adverse movements in stock price, bond ratings, revenues, profits, or liquidity ratios

- Indications from monitoring of performance that the quality of service is below established standards

Peterson also recommends that organizations consider whether the contract should allow termination for convenience—without cause. For example, termination for convenience can be an important solution when the organization must restructure, downsize, or reduce the scope of the project through no fault of the vendor—or when the outsourcing engagement is going miserably, but you simply cannot prove that the vendor is at fault. Vendors may agree to allow you to terminate a contract early provided you offer them proper notice and pay a termination for convenience fee. Negotiated precontract, these fees can be limited to reimbursement of reasonable costs experienced by the vendor (for example, any financial investments that the vendor made specifically to provide your service). Without suitable exit provisions, the for-convenience fee can become a request for an outrageous sum, with the vendor possibly claiming rights to all revenues it would have received during the entire term of the contract. If an organization decides to terminate the vendor contract early without cause, it is reasonable that the vendor recover the costs associated with the original contract; it is unreasonable that it receive unearned revenues or profits. The easiest method of staying within the bounds of what is reasonable is to negotiate these issues as part of the contract.

Peterson recommends that outsourcing contracts permit termination for convenience, addressing the following:

- When for convenience termination will be permitted (for example, only after the first full year)

- Partial termination (as in Example 3)

- Purchase of the vendor's unamortized assets that had been dedicated to providing services to the organization

By considering all of the events that might lead you to terminate your outsourcing agreement, for cause or convenience, you can design an outsourcing contract that will provide you with the exit rights you need.

TERMINATION ASSISTANCE

Termination assistance is another important part of any outsourcing contract. Since making the transition out of an outsourcing engagement may involve substantial risk to your organization, it is important to define a smooth and effective method to transfer your work to another vendor or to bring the outsourced function back in-house. The organization will want the vendor to provide adequate resources to effect a systematic and orderly transition at a reasonable price. Adding a contractual provision calling for the vendor to provide specific termination assistance will become the foundation for a clear exit management plan. Peterson refers to termination assistance as an "unwind provision," and he recommends that the termination assistance section include, for example,

- Transition planning assistance

- The obligation of the vendor to cooperate with the organization and replacement vendors

- Inventories of equipment, software, and other assets that the service provider uses to provide the services

- A minimum period during which the vendor will continue to perform base services if the organization requests it

- Transition services to be provided by the vendor and pricing for such services (for example, training)

- The right to solicit and hire the vendor's personnel who perform services for the organization

- The right to obtain the organization's data and other intellectual property in formats useful to the organization (data, procedures, error logs, documentation), along with the right to provide this information to potential successor vendors

- Consulting services in connection with the transition

- Parallel processing for some period, with the right to extend the term as necessary to resolve issues before the final cutover to the new service provider or in-house personnel

- Continued use of shared networks or other similar assets after the completion of the transaction

BUILT FOR EXIT

To cover the possibility that your service provider becomes unable to continue to deliver the contracted services to the organization, Peterson recommends that you consider a "built-for exit" provision in your contract. For example, without a built-for exit provision, should your service provider file for bankruptcy and become unable to provide termination assistance, the vendor may be allowed to avoid or stay (set aside) any of your claims for termination assistance. Under those circumstances, how would your organization seamlessly transfer the work to another provider or back in-house?

A built-for exit contract provision might require the service provider to

- Continue to use facilities, software, and equipment owned by the organization

- Continue to use subcontractors that the organization has a right to use

- Provide the organization with contact information for the vendor's key personnel

- Implement a disaster recovery plan if the vendor's facility were to be destroyed

- Cooperate with the organization in the creation of internal capabilities or other relationships to provide the same services that the vendor offered

While using these alternatives can lead to the loss of some of the economic benefits of outsourcing, in certain circumstances a built-for exit provision may be the only way to protect the organization effectively. For example, requiring that the vendor use the organization's facilities and technology may mean losing the benefit of the vendor's more advanced technology. However, losing the benefit of superior technology or economies of scale is far less dangerous than losing everything because of the vendor's bankruptcy.

Build your right to terminate into the contract in advance of the vendor's bankruptcy.

CONCLUSION

Without an exit strategy, you are locked in. The best time to address your exit management strategy is during due diligence, before the execution of the contract. Once the outsourcing contract has been signed, your negotiating leverage with your outsourcing vendor is significantly diminished.

Smart organizations think through all aspects of contract termination before signing the outsourcing contract. Well-written contracts include specific rights to terminate for cause or for convenience and include specific rights to termination assistance, including built for exit provisions. Knowledgeable executives work with outsourcing legal experts to create these provisions, and to retain control and preserve important alternatives and options for managing the exit from an outsourcing contract that ceases to be productive.

PART 5

NO SURPRISES

The goal of this book is to help you identify whether outsourcing is the right strategic business move for you and to give you the steps to take to make your outsourcing initiative succeed. If you apply the concepts and strategies discussed in this book, you will significantly decrease the risks of failure and dramatically increase your opportunities for success.

Going into an outsourcing initiative completely informed—that is, with your eyes wide open—will eliminate any real surprises during your decision, selection, transition, and ongoing management processes. In the following chapters, you will find a review of the most vital outsourcing success factors, along with resources that you can use today to ensure your success.

CHAPTER 14

SUCCESS FACTORS FOR OUTSOURCING

Whether on- or offshore, successful outsourcing initiatives are strategic business moves, tailored to fit your organization and your goals. We know that there is no one-size-fits-all when it comes to outsourcing; success factors for a manufacturing group may not be the same as success factors for a service organization, and big-company success factors may not spell success for midsized companies. So, with all the elements to consider when embarking on this outsourcing highway, what are the key components of success? Based on all of the research, the following are the key success factors for outsourcing, whether across the street or across the globe.

1. UNDERSTAND WHY YOU ARE GOING DOWN THIS ROAD IN THE FIRST PLACE

As Dick LeFave, CIO of Nextel, asked, "Why do it at all?" Successful outsourcing begins with a clear understanding of why you will outsource and a clear understanding of when outsourcing is, and when it is not, a smart business practice.

Since circumstances vary considerably from company to company and industry to industry, the decision to outsource must be an inside job. Conduct a risk and readiness assessment. If you are outsourcing to improve your business, you are on the right track, but the leadership must take the time to identify a compelling and quantifiable business reason to outsource. Only then can the best solution be found.

2. CHOOSE THE FUNCTIONS TO OUTSOURCE CAREFULLY

When considering which functions or departments to outsource, do not consider any failing or broken functions, hoping that once they are outsourced, they will be repaired—instead, the function or process will remain broken, and it will be miles away from your control. Fix any broken processes before outsourcing them, and move only those noncore functions or processes that will improve your business, your return on investment, and your customer loyalty.

Carefully evaluate any customer-facing activities that you choose to outsource by viewing them first through the eyes of your customers. After assessing the function through your customers' eyes, build specific customer-facing processes, conduct appropriate pilot testing, and manage your customers' experience closely *prior* to locking the organization into a long-term contract. In addition to using typical operational metrics as key performance indicators, work with your vendor to create key performance metrics on customer satisfaction and other quality-based measurements.

The bottom line is: If your customers will receive better, faster, or cheaper products and services as a result of your outsourcing initiative, then consider it. If your customers will be adversely affected, remember the customer satisfaction → customer loyalty → shareholder value concept from

Chapter 12. Outsourcing to improve business and reduce costs at the risk of losing customers makes no sense at all.

3. THOUGHTFUL VENDOR SELECTION

Once you have identified your compelling business reason to outsource and what functions can be outsourced well, take your time to select a vendor partnership that looks beyond cost drivers. Remember that outsourcing itself is not strategic, but your business goals are, so direct this vendor-selection process based on more than just sales presentations. Look carefully at references, synergy, opportunity for growth (scalability), a great team, financial stability, and flexibility.

Be prepared to test-drive the process (prove the concept). It is critical that the vendor you have selected and the program you are purchasing work for your organization.

"Outsourcing is a corporate strategic decision.
Organizations unable to articulate their decision
to outsource a function in this way
are doing it for the wrong reason."
—RUSS FAIRCHILD, CLIENT PARTNER, NETWORKINGPS, LLC
(FORMER GENERAL MANAGER, CHASE OUTSOURCING SERVICES)

---

4. COMMITMENT AND BUY-IN

With any outsourcing initiative, it is critical to get the support of all internal groups, and that support must begin at the top. Successful outsourcing initiatives are led by executives who understand and support the implementation of the entire lengthy, closely controlled outsourcing development methodology. Beginning with a strong business strategy, savvy and successful executives support the planning, defining of delivery standards, RFI and RFP process, vendor evaluation and selection, contract development and negotiation, communication process, and development of an all-inclusive governance model. This is a comprehensive process that is likely to take months; take your time.

In addition to executive management buy-in, in order for this process to deliver rewards, the organization must commit skilled resources, internal and external, with a shared vision and a clear understanding of the organization's strategy, goals, and objectives. The full potential of your outsourcing initiative can be realized only if the entire organization adopts a positive and supportive perspective throughout the entire often slow, sometimes frustrating process.

5. BUILD FIRST-CLASS TEAMS

The vendor selection and operations management teams must be supportive, knowledgeable, and capable of learning quickly. They must be flexible, collaborative, and future-focused. The operations management team must continue to focus on the business vision while managing change, relationships, trust and control, and results and aligning actions with business strategies. Select the very best team members based on the technical and behavioral skills required to succeed. Select project managers with sound leadership and project management skills, and with the ability to effectively integrate your outsourcing team with your in-house team. You must have the best teams, give them the best tools and skills, and work with them to ensure success.

6. COMMUNICATION

Much of the success of your outsourcing strategy will be generated by your teams, and a best-practice tip for increasing productivity during this change in organizational dynamics is through communication. The senior executive and manager responsible for the outsourcing program should communicate the organization's goals to employees and to prospective outsourcing vendors.

Far too many outsourcing programs fail because of a lack of communication. Be honest and frank about your outsourcing planning, especially as it relates to the organization's strategic business goals. Communicate honestly, early, and often.

7. QUALITY: A RETURN TO VALUE

Focus on quality throughout the outsourcing process, from strategic planning through ongoing management of the initiative:

- During the *decision to outsource* process, build a business case and assess your readiness for outsourcing with an eye on quality. Your current quality level may be adequate; make sure your service or product quality (and your reputation) will be improved through outsourcing.

- During the *vendor-selection* process, benchmark your current processes and assess your prospective vendors against your current performance on the basis of cost, time, and quality. Set policies, standards, and quality requirements that point to business improvement.

- During the *transition* process, quality means planning first, then implementing. Design the transition in stages with a reasonable timeline, work closely to manage the change in-house and with your vendor, manage the conflicts and the trouble spots as they occur, communicate clearly and often, and follow your governance model.

- During the *ongoing management* process, true up regularly to verify quality in process and delivery against your expectations, and be prepared for bumps in the road. Renegotiate if necessary, and balance control, flexibility, and trust.

- During the *exit* process, while quality (or lack of quality) may be the driver of the exit plan, use your own quality standards to evaluate your exit options before terminating your agreement. A well-written contract will provide the stepping-stones for a smooth exit if that is needed.

To maximize performance, manage an outsourcing initiative effectively, and provide your customers with world-class products and services; dedicate your entire organization to quality in every aspect of your outsourcing business model.

8. RELATIONSHIPS

In order to build and maintain strong vendor relationships, both parties must understand each other's core values and business models, and both parties must deliver on their promises. In addition,

- The organization must assign and empower the appropriate teams (selection, transition, and ongoing management) at the appropriate stage of the outsourcing project. This is not a part-time assignment for any team; give the team members full-time assignments to make your project successful.

- Focus on both metrics and people. Plan to go there for visits, have the vendor's employees visit you, and facilitate ongoing and frequent communication between your vendors, outsourcing team, and managers.

- To reap the full benefits of your outsourcing initiative, take the time to smooth out the transition process and put the appropriate control and governance mechanisms in place.

- Regularly true up with your vendor to measure achievement of goals, including productivity, performance, customer satisfaction, process, financial, and relationship goals, and quickly address anything that does not measure up.

- Celebrate your mutual achievements.

- Make sure that your entire organization supports your outsourcing team, and share your organizational vision, plans, and business model with your vendor to help it help you. Communicate often (this cannot be overstated), providing clear methods for feedback and follow-up between outsourcing and in-house managers and teams.

- Think through the opportunities for growth and improvement along with any potential bumps in the road (longterm and short-term) to anticipate changes, scope creep, or additional costs, and to evaluate the delivery performance of your vendor.

- No secrets equals no surprises.

9. RESULTS FOCUS

Managers in the old world order managed *processes*. Managers in the new world order manage *results*. Managers must learn how to focus on results in order to take advantage of the benefits of outsourcing. If you focus on processes, you are simply telling your outsourcer how to do its job—and that is not why you hired it. Let the vendor focus on the *how*; your organizational focus is on the *what*.

10. LEADERSHIP

In addition to commitment and buy-in, a successful outsourcing engagement requires every executive and manager to demonstrate leadership skills beyond those required by a typical hierarchical organizational structure. Partnering with an outsourcing service vendor requires a new level of collaboration, communication, negotiation, probing skills, critical thinking skills, business acumen, and mastery of change for the organization. An outsourcing initiative is no place for office politics; if you have a highly politically charged organization, work with an executive coach to eliminate that cultural hurdle. True leadership is about *what* is right, not *who* is right.

CHAPTER 15

RESOURCES FOR SUCCESS

This book was written to provide you with enough information to make initial decisions, and to point out that when you are ready to make your move, bringing in the right resources will facilitate your success. The experts quoted in the book are a great starting point for your own research, so feel free to contact them and take advantage of their research and recommendations.

VENTORO.COM:
OFFSHORE OUTSOURCING EXPERTISE

If you are planning to outsource offshore, you will want to speak with Ventoro's president, Phillip J. Hatch, early on. Ventoro was founded by executives from the offshore outsourcing market who recognized the incredible struggles that U.S. and European firms go through in defining, implementing, and managing offshore outsourcing strategies. While Ventoro works primarily with U.S. and European executives in defining sound offshore outsourcing strategies, it also works with companies around the globe to implement, manage, and optimize their outsourcing strategy. Using a combination of proprietary tools, seasoned analysts, and thorough research, Ventoro helps organizations through the entire offshore life cycle.

Ventoro's research study entitled "Offshore 2005 Research, Preliminary Findings and Conclusions" contains an incredible amount of valuable research for companies considering the offshore outsourcing option. A copy of the report is available online at www.ven toro.com. From this home page, simply click on the link to research and publications, where you can download your copy.

BRAD PETERSON:
LEGAL EXPERTISE FOR OUTSOURCING

With an office of over 50 attorneys specializing in outsourcing, Brad Peterson, a partner in Mayer, Brown, Rowe & Maw in Chicago, is himself a best practice in making your outsourcing initiative succeed. Clients look to Peterson and his staff to evaluate, structure, negotiate, and project-manage all types of outsourcing transactions, from relatively simple single-source transactions to more complex competitively bid multinational transactions.

A graduate of Harvard Law School (with honors), Peterson has worked with an impressive list of clients in outsourcing initiatives, onshore and off, and he is the author of a remarkable number of publications on the subject of outsourcing. His work "Outsourcing: Maximizing Value and Avoiding Pitfalls" is a must-read for anyone considering an outsourcing program; it is available by contacting Mr. Peterson's office via the Web (www.mayerbrown-rowe.com).

GEOFF SMITH:
EXPERIENCED OUTSOURCING
EXECUTIVE AND CONSULTANT

Geoff Smith, recently retired deputy chief information officer (CIO) of Procter & Gamble, has founded LP Enterprises, a consulting practice providing information technology, strategy, and customer relationship management expertise to his clients.

Smith is a true "hands-on" expert in the field of outsourcing, having taken P&G through the lengthy and successful process of determining what to outsource, the best strategy, the best vendors, and the best management of the transition and ongoing teams. Now Smith provides expert advice to other organizations to help them create the same success. He can be reached by e-mail: geoff.smith@fuse.net .

GEORGE SPAFFORD:
IT AUDIT, PROCESS IMPROVEMENT,
AND GOVERNANCE

George Spafford of Spafford Global Consulting is a much-sought-after consultant on IT audit, process improvement, and overall governance. He is an experienced IT practitioner and has held a variety of positions in IT operations, development, and management.

Spafford is a prolific author on a wide range of topics, including project management, technology business, communication, and security. He coauthored *The Visible Ops Handbook: Starting ITIL in Four Practical Steps* and, more recently, *Visible Ops: Positive Control Environment*, which steps an IT organization through the implementation of a control framework that properly mitigates risk and adds value. His e-mail newsletter, the *Daily News*, is filled with articles and resources in the areas affecting IT, including compliance, process improvement, human error, outsourcing, quality management, security, and more. The *Daily News* is available through Spafford's Web site, www.spaffordconsulting.com.

DAVID D'INNOCENZO: NETWORKINGPS

NetworkingPS is a midsize professional services firm founded in 2001 that specializes in planning, designing, assessing, implementing, and supporting systems, applications, and networks in multivendor environments. Building on its core competencies in software, systems, networks, and services, NetworkingPS provides a wide range of information-processing solutions.

David J. D'Innocenzo, president, CEO, and founder of NetworkingPS, provides what he calls "thought leadership" to his clients through this professional services firm. The ability to stay ahead of industry trends—to understand shifts in customer expectations and new technologies—is fundamental to the firm's ability to guide its clients to the right solutions. By bringing together the industry's best minds and most experienced resources, NetworkingPS and its customers have benefited from the interaction and shared experiences that occur during projects that have looked beyond the present, beyond the technology, to the bigger-picture visions of the future. More information on NetworkingPS can be found on their Web site, www.networkingps.com.

DR. ADAM KOLAWA:
PARASOFT

Parasoft is the leading provider of innovative solutions that automatically identify software errors and prevent them from recurring in the development and quality assurance process. Adam Kolawa, a Cal Tech Ph.D., founded Parasoft with four of his colleagues in 1987. Now CEO of Parasoft, Dr. Kolawa is an expert in the field of outsourcing, and is a well-known writer and speaker on industry issues. He has been granted 15 patents for the first parallel computer and numerous application development software products. He developed Automated Error Prevention ™, a methodology that not only detects software errors but also intuitively and automatically prevents the same errors from occurring again. Additional information on their automated software error prevention systems are available on their Web site, www.parasoft.com.

BINOD TATERWAY:
BLUE CANOPY

Blue Canopy is a pioneer in aligning business with information technology. Known for solving some of the toughest problems facing the IT industry, Blue Canopy focuses on business and technology interdependencies. Binod Taterway, a principal partner of Blue Canopy, is a recognized innovator in the field of business technology integration. Taterway has designed and delivered solutions that have guided such organizations as Marriott, General Motors, and Nextel to increased performance and efficiencies, while improving revenues and business value related to their IT enterprises. Taterway developed the Blue Canopy proprietary methodology entitled 4pi™ (fourth-party integrator), which helps CIOs manage vendors and service supply chains more effectively. Additional information on Taterway, Blue Canopy, and their products and services can be found on their Web site, www.blue-canopy.com.

SCOTT NOBEL:
GLOBAL SOURCING INSIGHTS

Global Sourcing Insights LLC (GSI) was formed by Scott Nobel and Ron Kreutzer, two senior managers from a large offshore outsourcing service provider. GSI advises organizations on using offshore outsourcing as a part of their business strategy. With combined experience of over 40 years, the team of Nobel and Kreutzer offers advisory services to organizations considering outsourcing as well as to service provider organizations.

Nobel, a contributor to this book in the area of culture and language, holds a master's degree in International Business from the University of Texas. Nobel is experienced in outsourcing best practices and has worked with Fortune 500 and Global 2000 firms on developing and implementing the processes that have come to define how global outsourcing is performed. He understands the need to integrate enhanced knowledge regarding people, cultures, political environments, and tax and regulatory regimes that affect global business and offshore outsourcing. To learn more about Nobel and GSI, go to www.gsinsights.com.

BRIAN MALONEY:
PEROT SYSTEMS

A former COO of Perot Systems, Maloney is now a consultant to organizations that want to improve their abilities through outsourcing. Maloney joined Perot Systems after 24 years with AT&T as senior vice president and president and CEO of AT&T Solutions, the networking professional services arm of AT&T Business. He was a member of the initial 12-person start-up team for AT&T Solutions, where he served as vice president of alliances and acquisitions. In 1995 he was appointed head of worldwide service delivery and managed the operations' vice presidents and general managers who led client engagement teams. In this capacity, he was responsible for all aspects of the teams' performance, including client satisfaction, financial results, revenue growth, and employee development.

Maloney was educated in New York, earning his bachelor's degree from Hunter College and a master's degree from Columbia University. He serves on the board of directors for the Thomas Edison State College Foundation and the New Jersey Intergenerational Orchestra. He also serves on the advisory board for Dow Jones Fiber Optic.

An outsourcing expert, Maloney can be reached through e-mail: brianmaloney@att.net.

MIKE MATTEO:
THREESIXTY SOURCING

ThreeSixty Sourcing provides solutions for every aspect of the supply chain for consumer and commercial products companies. Its mission statement is "to multiply the value of our customers' businesses by providing the world's best product sourcing solution for consumer and commercial hard goods." Mike Matteo, senior vice president, sourcing and operations for ThreeSixty, brings 20 years of experience in supply-chain and operations leadership with consumer goods companies and is a great resource for hard goods enterprises considering an offshore program. Matteo can be reached through ThreeSixty's Web site, www.360sourcing.com.

ART SALYER:
TROJAN BATTERIES

Art Salyer is executive vice president of operations for Trojan Battery Company and an inexhaustible contributor to this book. In his role with Trojan Batteries, Salyer has taken on the task of overseeing all manufacturing, distribution, logistics, engineering, quality, and customer care. Although he is based in California, Salyer frequently travels to Trojan's other facilities to manage their outsourcing projects with team members worldwide.

Before coming to Trojan, Salyer worked at companies such as Carttronics LLC, Creative Computers, Inc., Avery Dennison, Van Leer Corporation, and PepsiCo. His extensive experience includes manufacturing cost reduction, plant and distribution center management, change management, Internet commerce/virtual manufacturing, global supply-chain optimization, business/operations turnarounds, Mexico/

Asia plant operations, people and organizational development, and engineering management/new products. Salyer is an expert in outsourcing hard goods and an avid networker. If you would like to learn more from Salyer about his outsourcing expertise, contact him through the Trojan Web site: www.trojan-battery.com.

DICK LEFAVE:
NEXTEL

Dick LeFave is currently the senior vice president and chief information officer for Nextel Communications, located in Reston, Virginia. He has responsibility for the strategic deployment of information technology resources throughout Nextel. He has over 30 years' experience in the field of IT and management, including over 15 years as a CIO with the Boston Company, Thomas Cook Travel, American Express, and Southern New England Telephone. Dick received a Bachelor of Science degree from Boston University, an MBA from the University of Puget Sound, Seattle, Washington, and a Master of Science in Systems from the University of Southern California. He has completed the Advanced Management Program at the Harvard Business School, and he resides with his wife, Linda, and three children in Guilford, Connecticut. More about LeFave and Nextel can be found on their Web site, www.nextel.com.

LILIA TSALALIKHIN:
LUXOFT SOFTWARE SERVICES

Lilia Tsalalikhin is vice president and CMO of Luxoft, heading up its strategic marketing and the implementation of innovative marketing programs. Tsalalikhin graduated Summa Cum Laude with a Master of Science in Applied Mathematics and Computer Engineering from the University of Fine Mechanics and Optics in Leningrad, USSR, and is also a graduate of the IBM/Wharton Marketing Program. She holds the position of honorary faculty member at Moscow University of Physics and Technology.

Luxoft works carefully with its clients to ensure that it is bringing value to the table by maintaining focus on its mission: helping customers design, develop, test, and manage the best software solutions. Luxoft is a member of the IBS Group, Russia's most successful IT enterprise. Long-term relationships with companies like Dell, Deutsche Bank, Boeing, IBM, and others have given Luxoft a solid knowledge base and the means to grow its vertical industry expertise. For more information, go to the Luxoft Web site, www.luxoft.com.

EXECUTIVE COACHING

Much of the success of your outsourcing initiative is based on *people*—their ability to understand and be understood, their ability to embrace change, their ability to build relationships, their ability to quickly learn and implement new skills, their ability to agree on a vision and mission and then work to make it happen. One of the most important components you can add to your outsourcing arsenal is a good team of executive coaches. For that, I recommend my own company, Executive Coaching and Resource Network, where formally trained coaching experts, all with executive-level business experience, are ready to work with your team to make the people side of your outsourcing initiative successful. For additional information, please visit our Web site, www.Executive-Coaching.com, or e-mail me directly: LindaD@Executive-Coaching.com.

CONCLUSIONS

So, you have made it this far, all the way to the end of this book! However, reaching this point is just the beginning of your journey. Remember, even though it has been around for years, outsourcing is still in its infancy. Like the miners of 1849 at Sutter's Mill, we are all pioneers, finding our way through complicated and sometimes uncharted land, trying to take our piece of that golden pie.

In this fascinating world of outsourcing, there are certainly new challenges to meet, new rules to be written, and new riches to be gained. All that is needed is an awareness of the opportunities for risk and success, a great team of internal and external experts, and the courage to begin.

APPENDIX

THE EFFECT OF OUTSOURCING AND OFFSHORING ON BLS PRODUCTIVITY MEASURES

March 26, 2004

Recent discussions about the extent of outsourcing and off-shoring in the American economy have raised questions about the possible impact of these practices on productivity measures. In order to understand the impact, it is necessary to understand the construction of productivity measures and to look at historical trends in the productivity series. Around 1990, output per hour or labor productivity in the business sector began growing at a faster rate than had been seen in the previous 17 years. Given that productivity measures tend to grow faster during the early stages of economic recovery, the faster growth rate was not widely viewed as unusual at the time.

What was unusual was that the rate of productivity growth accelerated even further beginning around 1995, when normally it would be expected to slow as the recovery matured. While several explanations have been suggested, most economists believed that firms were finally able to harness the information technology revolution to introduce new methods of production, management controls, and services. This view, sometimes called the New Economy Paradigm, argued that a new, permanently higher trend rate of productivity growth has occurred. Others cautioned that another explanation might hold or that the effect of information technology might not be permanent.

The recession of 2001 seemed to further confirm the higher trend growth rate. While labor productivity growth did slow in 2001 compared to the previous five years, its growth was still rapid when compared to most other recessions. Productivity growth tends to be higher than average in recoveries, but coming out of the 2001 recession, business-sector productivity growth advanced at its fastest rate since 1950 and maintained its rapid rate during 2003, including the dramatic 9.4 percent annual growth rate reported for the third quarter.

Consequently, we have experienced nearly 13 years of faster productivity growth. While a number of explanations have been put forth, and to this list some have added measurement issues related to outsourcing and offshoring, any set of explanations should cover not just the last few years, but the entire 13-year period.

The Bureau of Labor Statistics (BLS) produces a family of productivity measures. For the purpose of understanding how offshoring might affect these measures, the key distinction is between those measures that include intersectoral intermediate inputs as part of the output measure and those that do not. Among those that include intermediates, multifactor productivity measures compare output trends to more than one input, and this framework can better help to trace the influence of offshoring on the productivity measures.

BUSINESS AND
NONFARM BUSINESS SECTOR

The quarterly measures of labor productivity, defined as output per hour, for the business and nonfarm business sectors utilize an output measure that is derived from the National Income and Product Accounts produced by the Bureau of Economic Analysis (BEA). Output is measured as the delivery of value-added to final demand, and so it does not include intermediate inputs. Imported finished goods and services to consumers reduce these output measures dollar for dollar.

Thus, outsourcing of production from manufacturing to domestic nonmanufacturing industries has little, if any, effect on measures of business and nonfarm business-sector output. Value-added has been shifted between the sectors, but the total value-added produced domestically is unchanged. If the outsourcing is from manufacturing to businesses located abroad ("offshoring"), business-sector output is lowered by the amount of value-added that is no longer produced in the United States. It does not matter for measurement purposes if offshoring is an intermediate product or service, such as a computer chip or call center services, or the entire production of a final product or service, such as a computer.

If it is assumed that an outsourced product or service is identical to the original, business-sector output is unaffected by outsourcing from one domestic industry to another. However, labor productivity can differ between the original manufacturer and the new outsourced producer. As a result, aggregate hours may rise or fall somewhat, but the effect on business-sector productivity will be quite modest.

In the case of offshoring, both business-sector output and hours will fall. Again, the net effect on business-sector labor productivity depends on the relative productivity of the lost output to the remaining output and any new output created. It is reasonable, however, to suppose that in this type of situation, lost production may have taken place in plants with relatively low levels of productivity. If so, then offshoring might raise labor productivity, but as with domestic outsourcing, the effect of this compositional effect is expected to be modest.

MANUFACTURING

For the quarterly manufacturing labor productivity series, the output concept is sectoral output, which is measured as the real value of shipments leaving the sector. Thus, this output measure includes intermediate inputs purchased from outside of the manufacturing sector. These intermediate inputs include materials, energy, and purchased business services, whether purchased from domestic or foreign suppliers. When output is compared to a single input, such as hours worked, productivity change also reflects the substitution of other inputs for labor.

Conceptually, the impact of offshoring is more pronounced in manufacturing measures than in the business-sector measures, provided the domestic manufacturer is purchasing the offshored goods or services as inputs. (As with the business sector, the complete loss of manufacturing production to an importer of finished goods leaves productivity largely unchanged.) If a domestic computer manufacturer switches from domestic to foreign suppliers of intermediate inputs, such as computer memory chips or call center services, real manufacturing sectoral output is unchanged because the real value of the computer is unchanged. Because U.S. jobs are lost (all other things unchanged), labor productivity will rise. If the U.S. manufacturer switches most of its production to offshore facilities, labor productivity might rise substantially.

While the labor productivity measures provide us with the most timely look at productivity trends, they do not provide us with the most comprehensive view. Multifactor productivity measures compare output to two or more inputs and remove from the labor productivity measures the effect of substitution among inputs. Within this framework, it is possible to account for labor productivity growth as the sum of multifactor productivity growth and the contribution of shifts in the mix of inputs. Table A.1 shows these data for manufacturing, where inputs include capital, hours, energy, materials, and purchased business services. Because these data are for manufacturing in its entirety, energy, materials, and purchased business services are purchased from the domestic nonmanufacturing sector or imported. Both outsourced and imported inputs are included, but they cannot be separately identified in these data.

The acceleration of labor productivity through 2000 is evident in Table A.1. The overwhelming portion of this acceleration comes from faster multifactor productivity growth, leaving little to be accounted for by capital deepening or domestic outsourcing or offshoring of materials and business services. In combination, increased use of materials and business services relative to labor contributes almost exactly the same amount in each of the earliest two periods and slows beginning in 1995. Therefore, domestic outsourcing and offshoring explain none of the labor productivity speed-up. While this does not preclude imports from representing a rising share of materials and business services, it suggests a limit to the scope of their influence

Table A.1 Sources of Labor Productivity Growth in Manufacturing, 1973–2001
(percent per year)

	1973–1990	1990–1995	1995–2000	2000–2001
Labor productivity	2.5	3.3	4.1	1.2
Equals:				
Multifactor productivity	0.5	1.2	2.3	–0.8
Plus:				
Input deepening				
Materials	1.0	1.0	0.7	1.1
Business services	0.4	0.5	0.2	–0.4
Energy	0.0	0.1	0.0	0.0
Capital	0.6	0.5	0.8	1.3

Multifactor productivity plus the effects of input deepening may not sum to labor productivity due to rounding. All data are reporting using the Standard Industrial Classification system.

Labor productivity measures are from the Multifactor Productivity Trends program and may not equal those reported in the quarterly Productivity and Costs news release.

Source: Multifactor Productivity Trends in Manufacturing, 2001, USDOL 04-148, February 10, 2004.

on productivity change. Because of data limitations, the manufacturing multifactor productivity measures are not yet available for years after 2001.

The final set of manufacturing data comes from the BLS international comparisons program, where labor productivity for manufacturing is measured as value-added output per hour worked. Value-added output is produced by the BEA. Value-added output measures the contribution of capital and labor to production and excludes intermediates. In this framework, outsourcing and offshoring have the same effect. Both output and hours fall, and, like the business sector, the net effect is likely to be slight. This is the case whether the lost production is an intermediate good or a final product.

Table A.2 provides a comparison of the Bureau's family of manufacturing measures. All three measures show an acceleration in the growth rate of productivity. The measure of value-added output per hour grew slightly faster than the sectoral output per hour measure. This implies that combined intermediates grew slightly more slowly than sectoral output. It can be inferred from the similar pattern of sectoral and value-added productivity growth that intermediates are not a primary explanation of the faster productivity growth.

SUMMARY

Productivity growth, however it is measured, accelerated in the 1990s, and this faster growth has continued on during the last recession and recovery. Offshoring affects business-sector productivity change only through changes in the composition of domestic production, and its effect is likely to be small. In

Table A.2 Comparison of Bureau of Labor Statistics' Productivity Measures in Manufacturing

(percent per year)

Period	Sectoral Output per Hour[1]	Multifactor Productivity[2]	Value-Added Output per Hour[3]
1979–1990	2.6	1.1	3.0
1990–1995	3.3	1.3	3.3
1995–2000	4.3	2.1	4.5
2000–2001	1.8	-0.8	0.4
2001–2002	6.5	N.A.	9.2 P
2003 1st quarter	5.8	N.P.	N.P.
2003 2d quarter	2.8	N.P.	N.P.
2003 3d quarter	9.0	N.P.	N.P.

All data are reporting using the Standard Industrial Classification system.

P—Based on preliminary value-added measures from the gross product originating program of the Bureau of Economic Analysis.

N.A.—Data are not available.
N.P.—Not produced. Only annual data are only available for these series.

1. Sectoral output per hour is the real value of shipments leaving an industry (including the value of intermediate inputs) divided by hours at work. Data are from the quarterly *Productivity and Costs News Release*, December 3, 2003.

2. Multifactor productivity is sectoral output per combined units of capital, hours at work, energy, nonenergy materials, and purchased business services. Data are from the annual *Multifactor Productivity Trends in Manufacturing*, 2001, USDOL 04-148, February 10, 2004.

3. Value-added output per hour is sectoral output *less* the real value of intermediate inputs (materials, energy, and purchased business services) per hour at work. Data are from the annual *International Comparisons of Manufacturing Productivity and Unit Labor Cost Trends*, March 26, 2004.

Source: Bureau of Labor Statistics.

manufacturing, the combination of domestic outsourcing and offshoring has contributed about 1.5 percent per year to sectoral output per hour growth through 1995, but only about 1 percent per year thereafter, and as a result, they do not appear to be an explanation for the productivity speed-up.

This conclusion must be qualified in two ways. First, there is no information on the relative importance of offshoring relative to domestic outsourcing, and so it is not known if foreign suppliers have become a growing substitute for domestic suppliers of intermediate inputs. Even if they have, under reasonable assumptions, offshoring appears to explain only a small fraction of the productivity speed-up. Second, not all BLS data extend beyond 2001, and so it cannot be ascertained if there has been a sudden shift in trends. Even if there has, the impact of outsourcing and offshoring on productivity change is likely to be small.

Outsourcing Fast Facts

1. Did you know that according to Gartner Research, a typical outsourcing initiative takes about nine months to get off the ground?

2. The U.S. Department of Labor, Bureau of Labor Statistics reports that outsourcing and offshoring of intermediate production don't necessarily inflate the government's productivity measurements.

   In the business sector, outsourcing to domestic non-manufacturing industries and offshoring to foreign businesses alter the distribution of production among firms. Since firms can differ in their productivity, domestic outsourcing can affect business sector productivity if the contracting firm differs in its

OUTSOURCING CHECKLIST

Stage	Purpose and Goal	Check points	Chapter Reference
Decision Team (DT)	**What to Outsource**	**1. Assign project manager**	**Chapter 4**
		2. Convene team of inside experts and senior management	
		3. Engage outside independent expert	
		4. Determine functions to be outsourced	
Vendor Selection Team (VST)	**Shop for vendors; develop success metrics**	**1. Convene a new team**	**Chapters 5 and 6**
		2. Assign VST Project Manager, exclusive to this project	
		3. Select outside expertise to support initiative, including independent outsource consultant and outsource attorney	
		4. Conduct research to identify appropriate potential vendors	
		5. Create Request for Information (RFI) to communicate your business needs	

6. Create request for proposal (RFP) asking for bids on a well-defined implementation strategy
7. Weigh results against predetermined parameters
8. Create transition plan
9. Create and implement communication plan
10. Create and implement comprehensive Service Level Agreement (SLA)
11. Create vendor-client agreement
12. Implement transition job

Ongoing Management Team (OMT)	Succeed	Chapters 7, 8. 9

1. **Convene new team**
2. Identify new skills needed
3. Implement communication strategy
4. Engage outside expertise to learn new skills
5. Set True-Up schedule; implement

productivity from the outsourced production. Similarly, offshoring can affect business sector productivity if the productivity of the production lost to offshoring differs from the productivity of remaining and any new U.S. business sector production. Any effect of offshoring on business sector productivity change is expected to be modest.

Outsourcing and offshoring have the potential for greater effect on labor productivity at the industry level. In manufacturing, outsourcing and offshoring have contributed about 1.5 percent per year to sectoral output per hour growth between 1973 and 1995. Their contribution has slowed to only about 1 percent per year thereafter and as a result they do not appear to be an explanation for the productivity speed-up in manufacturing.

Further discussion can be found in "The Effect of Outsourcing and Offshoring on Productivity Change," attached as an appendix.

2. It's no secret that outsourcing will be one of the fastest-growing segments of the U.S. Federal IT budget over the next five years. According to a December 2004 report entitled "Federal Outsourcing MarketView," created by INPUT, a research agency (www.input.com), Federal IT outsourcing will grow 55 percent, from $11.7 billion in fiscal year 2004 to $17.4 billion in fiscal year 2009, representing a compound annual growth rate (CAGR) of close to 8.3 percent.

3. About 54 percent of the population of India is under the age of 25; the cost of living in India is 20 percent of that in the United States.

4. The total value of outsourcing to India in June 2005 was estimated at $17.2 billion, or 44 percent of the worldwide total, according to a report from India's National Association of Software and Service Companies (Nasscom).

5. According to research conducted in 2003, relative wages of manufacturing employees (wages only; no benefits) as a percentage of U.S. wages were as follows:

Europe		Asia		Americas	
Romania	4%	Vietnam	2%	Colombia	6%
Bulgaria	6%	China	3%	Argentina	7%
Slovakia	9%	India	4%	Venezuela	10%
Russia	11%	Philippines	6%	Chile	17%
Czech Republic	15%	Malaysia	8%	Mexico	23%
Hungary	18%	Thailand	10%	Brazil	21%
Turkey	20%	Indonesia	15%	Canada	91%
Portugal	23%	Hong Kong	32%		
Slovenia	38%	Korea	33%		
United Kingdom	81%	Taiwan	37%		
Sweden	88%	Singapore	59%		
France	91%	New Zealand	53%		
Italy	105%	Australia	66%		
Norway	117%	Japan	68%		

1. Dmitry Loschinin, president and CEO of Russia's premier outsourcing firm, Luxoft (www.luxoft.com), says that the number-one point executives should know

when considering an outsourcing initiative is this: The decision to outsource is a strategic decision that should be driven by more than a need to save money. Executives must have a clear understanding of why, what, where, and with whom to outsource prior to finalizing a decision. Key factors shouldn't be lowest labor costs but vital factors such as supplier technical expertise, strength of management, organizational capabilities, cultural fit, language skills, and commitment to quality, as well as task complexity and suitability for outsourcing.

2. A survey of 45 companies known to outsource at least one function, conducted by the Earth Institute at Columbia University, showed that of the 82 percent of the respondents that were currently outsourcing jobs, 79 percent of them were outsourcing to offshore businesses. The majority of respondents reported better competitive prices and improved work skills. (As reported in the *Earth Institute News*, July 22, 2004, by Jill Stoddard (js2372@columbia.edu).

3. When outsourcing crosses paths with Sarbanes-Oxley, additional costs—related to reporting requirements— may be incurred. While the party responsible for those costs is a point of negotiation, SOX is another reason to accurately define the service-level agreement and reporting requirements with your outsourcing vendor.

INDEX

A.T. Kearney, 195
Abbreviations, 2–3
Above-the-line behaviors, 132
Accenture, 39–40
Access to world-class capabilities, 41
Accountability, 34, 131–132
Achieved-status culture, 156–157
Acronyms, 2–3
Adaptability, 133
ADP, 5–6
Adult learning, 115–117
Affiliative leadership style, 107
Airline industry, 39–40
Andragogy, 115
Ascribed-status culture, 1 57, 156
Asian manufacturing wages, 219
A.T. Kearney, 195
Automated error prevention, 199
Automatic Data Processing (ADP), 5–6

Balancing stakeholders' needs, 161–169
   customer value, 166–167
   employee value, 164–165
   shareholder value, 162–164
   stakeholder expectations, 168–169
   vendor value, 165–166
Barriers to success. *See* Outsourcing
   hurdles
Baseball, 135
Basic do's and don'ts, 57–58
Below-the-line behaviors, 132
Blogging, 127
BLS productivity measures, 208–215
Blue Canopy, 60, 199–200
Brain drain, 138–140
Breakeven point, 105

Built for exit contract provision, 180–182
Bureau of Labor Statistics (BLS)
   productivity measures, 208–215
Business activities matrix, 53–56
Business experts. *See* Resources for success
Business focus, 38–39
Business sector productivity, 209–210
Butler, Nicholas Murray, 110

Call center employees, 152
Capital funds, 42–43
Career path, 113
Cash infusion, 42
Chain of command, 157
Change agents, 118
Change management, 78–80, 88, 114–119
Chevy Nova - Latin American market, 147
Chief information officer (CIO), 12
Coaching leadership style, 107–108
Coercive leadership style, 106–107
Cohen, Linda, 48, 62, 63, 77, 112, 124,
   195–196
College training program, 140
Communication
   culture, 155
   resistance to change, 81–83
   risk, as, 35
   online communication lines, 126–127
   success factor, as, 189
   trust building, 125
Communications plan, 81
Company size (level the playing field), 41
Competitive bidding process, 66–72
Conflict management, 129–130
Contract termination. *See* Exit management
Core competencies, 56

Corporate hierarchical system, 156
Cost savings, 20, 22, 23
Cultural barriers, 147–158
 culture, 153–156
 language, 151–153
 status, 156–157
 time zone differences, 148–151
Culture, 153–156
Customer-facing activities, 51–53
Customer-facing service, 46
Customer satisfaction, 143–144, 167
Customer service risks, 30
Customer value, 166–167

Daily News, 198
Decision management, 119
Decision team, 48–49
Delivery deadlines, 33
Delivery risks, 32–34
Democratic leadership style, 107
Demographic dynamics, 25
Describing services, 87
Dias, Gina, 149
D'Innocenzo, David J., 85, 198
Disaster recovery, 36–37, 88–89
DISC, 78
Disney, Roy, 45
Dragnet provisions, 87
Due diligence, 38, 56

E-mail, 154
Earth Institute survey (Columbia
 University), 220
"Effect of Outsourcing and Offshoring on
 Productivity Change, The," 207–215
Employee bitterness, 36
Employee perception, 100
Employee skill base, 99–100
Employee value, 164–165
Engineering, 25
English language, 151
Ethical issues, 38
 ethical expert, 196
 protection of sensitive/personal
 information, 136–138
 transition period, 80
European manufacturing wages, 219
Exclusivity, 87–88
Executive buy-in, 145–146
Executive coaching, 204–205
Executive Coaching and Resource
 Network, 204–205

Exit management, 171–182
 alternative options, 176
 built for exit provision, 180–182
 for cause exit provision, 177–179
 for convenience, 177–179
 example vignettes, 171–173
 questions to ask, 174–175
 reasons for exiting, 177–178
 termination assistance, 179–180
Expert interviewees. *See* Resources for
 success

Failures, 10–11, 23–25
Fairchild, Russ, 187
Fast facts (factoids), 215–219
Fear, uncertainty, and doubt (FUD), 79, 94
Federal IT outsourcing, 218
"Federal Outsourcing Market View," 218
Feedback and support, 130–131
First 90 Days (Watkins), 105
Fixed/variable-cost situation, 39
Flu vaccine, 37
For cause exit contract provision,
 177–179
For convenience termination, 177–179
Force majeure events, 177
4pi (fourth-party integrator), 60, 200
Friedrich, Rick, 27
FUD, 79, 94

Gandhi, Mahatma, 120
Gartner, Inc., 41, 195–196
Global Sourcing Insights (GSI), 200–201
Gold Rush, 17–18
Goleman, Daniel, 106
Good performance index, 103
Growth, 33

Hatch, Phillip J., 17–19, 21–24, 51, 52,
 67–72, 81, 82, 106, 193
Hierarchical system (U. S. corporations),
 156
Hot line, 150
How to Shine at Work (Dominguez), 100
Hurdles. *See* Outsourcing hurdles

India, 218–219
Information technology capabilities, 87
INPUT, 218
Instant messaging (IM), 127
Interviewees. *See* Resources for success
IT capabilities, 87

Joint problem solving, 96

Kelly, William Russell, 6
Kelly Services, 6–7
Knowledge integration, 127–128
Knowledge retention, 139
Kolawa, Adam, 49–51, 199
Kreutzer, Ron, 200–201

Labor productivity, 209–218. *See also*
    Productivity measures
Labor shortage, 25
Lack of communication, 155
Language, 151–153
Laudicina, Paul, 25, 195
Leadership skills, 108–111, 120–121
Leadership style, 106–108
"Leadership That Gets Results"
    (Goleman), 106
Leading by example, 109, 120
Learned Optimism (Seligman), 109
Learning, 133–134
LeFave, Dick, 72–73, 81, 111, 140,
    185, 203
Legal issues, 37–38
    exit management. *See* Exit management
    legal expert, 194
    rules and regulations, 34
    transition period, 89
Locked in, 175–176
Loschinin, Dmitry, 219
LP Enterprises, 197
Luxoft, 203–204, 219

Major-league baseball, 135
Maloney, Brian, 12, 153, 201
Management skills, 111–121
    change management, 114–119
    decision management, 119
    risk management, 113–114
    strategic management, 119–120
Manager, 123–134
    accountability, 131–132
    adaptability, 133
    communication, 125, 126–127
    conflict management, 129–130
    feedback and support, 130–131
    knowledge integration, 127–128
    learning, 133–134
    online communication techniques,
        126–127
    results management, 123–124

Manager (*Cont.*):
    skills. See Management skills
    traits, 134
    trust building, 124–125, 132–133
    united front, 125–126
    visiting the vendor, 128–129
Manufacturing productivity, 210–214
Manufacturing wages, 219
Matteo, Mike, 118, 145, 202
Measure, monitor, and report (MMR),
    110–111
Meetings, 130
Mentoring, 140
Midsize organizations, 41
Miracle-Gro, 27
Mission statement, 102–103
MMR process, 110–111
Motivation, 109
Multifactor productivity, 214

NetworkingPS, 198–199
New economy paradigm, 208
Nextel Communications, 72,
    140, 203
Nobel, Scott, 154–156, 163, 200–201
North American manufacturing wages,
    219

Obstacles to success. *See* Outsourcing
    hurdles
Office politics, 192
Offshoring, 5, 7
OK, IF stage of resistance, 79
OMT, 77, 97–98. *See also* Team/team
    building
Ongoing feedback and support, 130–131
Online communication techniques,
    126–127
Operating costs, 39–40
Operations management team (OMT), 77,
    97–98. *See also* Team/team building
Optimism, 97, 109–110
Organizational responsibilities, 161
Output measurement, 209, 214
Outsourcing
    advantages, 9
    checklist, 216–217
    cost savings, 22, 23
    defined, 5
    do's and dont's, 57–58
    failures, 10–11, 23–25
    fast facts (factoids), 215–219

Outsourcing (*Cont.*):
hurdles, 135–146. *See also* Outsourcing hurdles
questions to ask, 14–15
reasons for, 8–9, 20–21
resources, 193–205. *See also* Resources for success
size of market, 19–20
success factors, 185–192
successes, 11–12, 22
tips/hints, 46
what to outsource, 45–58. *See also* What to outsource
"Outsourcing: Maximizing Value and Avoiding Pitfalls" (Peterson), 86, 194
Outsourcing checklist, 216–217
Outsourcing experts. *See* Resources for success
Outsourcing fast facts, 215–219
Outsourcing hurdles, 135–146
brain drain, 138–140
cultural barriers, 147–158. *See also* Cultural barriers
customer satisfaction, 143–144
ethics, 136–138. *See also* Ethics
executive buy-in, 145–146
philosophical differences, 143
salespeople vs. executive, 140–141
scalability, 144–145
scope creep, 141–142
Outsourcing team (decision team), 48–49
Oz Factor, The (Connor et al.), 131

Pacesetting leadership style, 107
Pain, 8
Parasoft, 199
Personality clash, 130
Peterson, Brad, 56, 65, 86, 89, 171, 174, 177–180, 194
Philosophical differences, 143
Pilot, 72
Political concerns, 37
Ponemon, Larry, 80, 136, 196
Ponemon Institute, 196
Power play, 8
Principles of adult learning, 116–117
Privacy and security risks, 31–32
Problem function, 9, 46
Process review, 56
Procter & Gamble (P&G), 13–14, 36
Productivity measures
business sector, 209–210

Productivity measures (*Cont.*):
effect of outsourcing, 215, 218
manufacturing, 210–214
Project manager, 46–48

Quality, 33, 189–190

Redirecting resources, 42
Regulations, 34
Relationship with vendor, 190–191
Request for information (RFI), 67
Request for proposal (RFP), 68, 70
Requirements contracts, 88
Resource availability, 87
Resources for success, 193–205
Blue Canopy, 199–200
Cohen, Linda, 195–196
executive coaching, 204–205
Laudicina, Paul, 195
LeFave, Dick, 203
Luxoft, 203–204
Maloney, Brian, 201
Matteo, Mike, 202
NetworkingPS, 198–199
Nobel, Scott, 200–201
Parasoft, 199
Peterson, Brad, 194
Ponemon, Larry, 196
Salyer, Art, 202–203
Smith, Geoff, 197
Spafford, George, 197–198
Ventoro.com, 193–194
Results focus, 192
Results management, 123–124
Rewards, 38–44. *See also* Risk–reward analysis
RFI, 67
RFP, 68, 70
Right-wrong orientation to knowing-learning continuum, 134–135
Risk management, 113–114
Risk-reward analysis, 29–44
access to world-class capabilities, 41
business focus, 38–39
capital funds, 42–43
cash infusion, 42
company size (level the playing field), 41
customer service risks, 30
delivery risks, 32–34
disaster recovery, 36–37
employee reaction, 35–36
ethical concerns, 38. *See also* Ethical issues

Risk-reward analysis (*Cont.*):
  legal concerns, 37–38. *See also* Legal
    issues
  noncompliance with rules/regulations,
    34
  operating costs, 39–40
  political concerns, 37
  privacy and security risks, 31–32
  redirecting resources, 42
Rulebook, 86
Rules and regulations, 34
Russell Kelly Office Services, 6

Salespeople *vs.* executive, 140–141
Salyer, Art, 46, 48, 151–153, 202–203
Sarbanes-Oxley Act (SOX), 34, 220
Scalability, 144–145
Science, 25
Scope creep, 33–34, 141–142
Scotts Company, 27
Sectoral output per hour, 214
Seligman, Martin, 109
Service level agreement (SLA), 83–85
Shareholder value, 162–164
Site visit, 70, 128
Skills, 105–121
  leadership, 108–111
  managers, 111–120. *See also Management
    skills*
  tips/hints, 120–121
SLA, 83–85
Slow-to-change tendency, 35
Smith, Geoff, 12–14, 135, 197
South American manufacturing wages, 219
SOX, 34, 220
Spafford, George, 53, 64, 168, 197–198
Stakeholder expectations, 168–169
Status, 156–157
Status quo approach to change, 78–79
Stoddard, Jill, 220
Strategic management, 119–120
Success factors for outsourcing, 185–192
  commitment/buy-in, 187–188
  communication, 189
  leadership, 192
  quality, 189–190
  relationships, 190–191
  results focus, 192
  team building, 188. *See also* Team/team
    building
  vendor selection, 187. *See also* Vendor
    selection

Success factors for outsourcing (*Cont.*):
  what to outsource, 186–187
  why outsourcing?, 185–186
Successes, 11–12, 22
Sutter, John, 17

Taterway, Binod, 60–62, 85–86, 199–200
Team/team building, 93–104
  basics, 93–94
  delivering results stage, 96–97
  getting to work stage, 96
  good performance index, 103
  honeymoon is over stage, 95–96
  honeymoon stage, 94–95
  how analysis, 102–103
  joint problem solving, 96
  mission statement, 102–103
  optimism, 97
  vision statement, 101–102
  what analysis, 98–101
  where analysis, 101–102
Team mission statement, 102–103
Terminating the relationship. *See* Exit
    management
Termination assistance, 179–180
Termination for convenience, 177–179
Termination for convenience fee, 177, 178
Threaded discussions, 126
ThreeSixty Sourcing, 202
Time-sharing, 29
Time zone differences, 148–151
Transition period, 75–90
  change management, 78–80, 88
  communicating with staff, 81–83
  describing services, 87
  disaster recovery, 88–89
  ethics, 80
  factors to consider, 75–76
  legal issues, 89
  OMT, 77
  rulebook, 86
  SLA, 83–85
  SMO, 86
  strategy, 76
Trojan Batteries, 202–203
True-ups, 73, 111
Trust/trust building, 120, 124–125,
    132–133
Tsalalikhin, Lilia, 165, 203–204

UCSF Med Center, 31
United front, 125–126

Value-added output, 213
Value-added output per hour, 214
Value-creating organizations, 163. *See also* Balancing shareholders' needs
Values, 46
Vendor performance measurement, 89
Vendor relationships, 190–191
Vendor selection, 59–74
  checklist, 71
  competitive bidding process, 66–72
  control framework, 64
  exclusivity, 87–88
  factors to consider, 60–62
  IT capabilities, 87
  performance evaluation, 89
  pilot, 72
  privacy concerns, 137–138
  RFI, 67
  RFP, 48, 70
  site visit, 70
  vendor selection team, 62–64
  working relationship, 65–66
Vendor selection checklist, 71
Vendor selection team, 62–64

Vendor value, 165–166
Ventoro.com, 8, 17, 20, 193–194
Visible Ops: Positive Control Environment (Spafford et al.), 197
Visible Ops Handbook: Starting ITIL in Four Practical Steps, The (Spafford et al.), 197
Vision statement, 101–102
Visiting the vendor, 128–129
Voice over IP (VoIP), 127

Wage comparisons, 219
Watkins, Michael, 105
Web conferencing, 127
"What Offshore Outsourcing Projects Fail" (Nobel), 154
What to outsource, 45–58
  business activities matrix, 53–56
  customer-facing activities, 51–53
  decision team, 48–49
  process review, 56
  project manager, 46–48
  three-step strategy, 49–51
World-class capabilities, 41
World Out of Balance (Laudicina), 25, 195

ABOUT THE AUTHOR

Linda Dominguez is the Principal of Executive Coaching and Resource Network, author of the best-selling book *How to Shine at Work* (McGraw-Hill), a Master Executive Coach, and a motivational speaker. With a background that includes over 25 years of corporate, consulting, and coaching experience, Linda provides individual and group coaching in the areas of leadership, business strategy, business development, executive development, and improved individual and corporate performance. Linda has worked with hundreds of Fortune 500 clients around the world to help them improve their bottom-line results, and find the right balance between professional success and personal fulfillment.

One of the most widely recognized coaches in the world, Linda has been featured in numerous magazines and newspapers throughout the United States, including the *Wall Street Journal, Fortune* magazine, *Latina* magazine, *CareerJournal.com, Black Enterprise* magazine, *HR* magazine, and *CFO* magazine, and she has appeared on several radio and television shows